Curating, Interpretation and Museums

Following a period of strategic and ideological change in museums, this book outlines new attitudes in curating and display, education and learning, text and interpretation, access, inclusion, participation, space, and issues around the sustainability of the encyclopaedic collection.

Focused on the contemporary period, the author questions the extent to which the museum visitor has become reliant on interpretative text and examines the development of new museum spaces where visitor interaction and engagement is welcomed. Changes of attitude have transformed our museums into modern spaces that reflect current needs and modern expectations and yet our permanent collections remain relatively unchanged, sometimes an uncomfortable reminder of a time when values, ethics, and attitudes were very different. The author will discuss these conflicts of ideology.

Written by a researcher with expertise in museum practice, this shortform book offers a new approach that will be valuable reading for students and scholars of cultural management and policy, as well as providing insights for reflective museum practitioners.

Sylvia Lahav is an associate lecturer at Goldsmiths, University of London, an independent museum consultant, researcher, and writer.

Routledge Focus on the Global Creative Economy
Series Editor: Aleksandar Brkić, *Goldsmiths, University of London, UK*

This innovative Shortform book series aims to provoke and inspire new ways of thinking, new interpretations, emerging research, and insights from different fields. In rethinking the relationship of creative economies and societies beyond the traditional frameworks, the series is intentionally inclusive. Featuring diverse voices from around the world, books in the series bridge scholarship and practice across arts and cultural management, the creative industries and the global creative economy.

Innovation in the Arts
Concepts, Theories, and Practices
Jason C. White

Creative Women in Ireland
Not Your Muse
Aileen O'Driscoll

Cultural Mediation for Museums
Driving Audience Engagement
Edited by Michela Addis, Isabella de Stefano and Valeria Guerrisi

Rethinking Cultural Centers
A Nordic Perspective on Multipurpose Cultural Organizations
Tomas Järvinen

Curating, Interpretation and Museums
When Attitude Becomes Form
Sylvia Lahav

For more information about this series, please visit: www.routledge.com/Routledge-Focus-on-the-Global-Creative-Economy/book-series/RFGCE

Curating, Interpretation and Museums
When Attitude Becomes Form

Sylvia Lahav

LONDON AND NEW YORK

First published 2023
by Routledge
4 Park Square, Milton Park, Abingdon, Oxon OX14 4RN

and by Routledge
605 Third Avenue, New York, NY 10158

Routledge is an imprint of the Taylor & Francis Group, an informa business

© 2023 Sylvia Lahav

The right of Sylvia Lahav to be identified as author of this work has been asserted in accordance with sections 77 and 78 of the Copyright, Designs and Patents Act 1988.

All rights reserved. No part of this book may be reprinted or reproduced or utilised in any form or by any electronic, mechanical, or other means, now known or hereafter invented, including photocopying and recording, or in any information storage or retrieval system, without permission in writing from the publishers.

Trademark notice: Product or corporate names may be trademarks or registered trademarks, and are used only for identification and explanation without intent to infringe.

British Library Cataloguing-in-Publication Data
A catalogue record for this book is available from the British Library

Library of Congress Cataloging-in-Publication Data
Names: Lahav, Sylvia, author.
Title: Curating, interpretation and museums : when attitude becomes form / Sylvia Lahav.
Description: Abingdon, Oxon ; New York, NY : Routledge, 2023. | Includes bibliographical references and index.
Identifiers: LCCN 2022057584 (print) | LCCN 2022057585 (ebook) | ISBN 9781032081410 (hardback) | ISBN 9781032081458 (paperback) | ISBN 9781003213130 (ebook)
Subjects: LCSH: Museums–Curatorship–Social aspects
Classification: LCC AM7 .L34 2023 (print) | LCC AM7 (ebook) | DDC 069.01–dc23/eng/20230203
LC record available at https://lccn.loc.gov/2022057584
LC ebook record available at https://lccn.loc.gov/2022057585

ISBN: 978-1-032-08141-0 (hbk)
ISBN: 978-1-032-08145-8 (pbk)
ISBN: 978-1-003-21313-0 (ebk)

DOI: 10.4324/9781003213130

Typeset in Times New Roman
by Newgen Publishing UK

Contents

	Introduction	1
1	Collecting, Exhibiting, and Curating	6
2	Interpretation and Text	30
3	Space and Place	45
4	The Will to Know	60
	Looking Back ... Final Thoughts	75
	Index	78

Introduction

The phrase, When Attitude Becomes Form has been in my head for a while now. Using it in my title is not intended to suggest that Harold Szeemann's iconic 1969 exhibition will be the sole focus of my book. Many journals, articles, and exhibitions have comprehensively examined and analysed the content, form, and structure of this important show. My use of the shortened and slightly adapted title is to signal the proposition I am making about attitudes that were adopted by those working in museums of art in the latter half of the twentieth century and how they have subsequently shaped the selection, display, and interpretation of art.

First, some clarifications. The word museum will be used in reference to museums of art, predominantly those that have both historic and modern collections. I will contrast the selection and display of work from the permanent collection with that of exhibition curating, which, since the 1990s has become an increasingly popular topic for books and journal papers. Very few books are devoted to the everyday care and management of the permanent collection. This is an area that interests me.

As my career of many years was in museums and galleries in London, Tate, the National Gallery, the National Portrait Gallery, and the Victoria and Albert Museum, most of my observations and research is taken from these cultural institutions (Tate in particular), but I hope that the broader discussion will be relevant to museums in other parts of the world. Finally, and most importantly, I see this book as an extension of my teaching, that is, to interrogate concepts, ask questions, and initiate debate rather than definitively answer and possibly restrict further discussion.

I will highlight areas where attitudes that were adopted in response to social, political, and educational change have become embedded in

DOI: 10.4324/9781003213130-1

2 *Introduction*

the structure and management of museums, influencing their form and function and often how work is interpreted and communicated too.

Outline of Chapters

In Chapter 1, I question whether newly configured notions of museum practice are reflected in methods of curating and overall professional, artistic, and cultural practice. I will refer to the way in which curators acquire work for the permanent collection and contrast this with the organisation of temporary exhibitions. I will suggest that these two interconnected roles have developed different characters, different modes of practice and different functions.

Some might say that our permanent collections languish in theoretical vacuums shrouded by narratives that are out of date, out of time, and largely irrelevant to our modern sensibilities, that some aspects of our permanent collections resemble older relatives or friends whose values and opinions evoke feelings of shame and embarrassment. Even if we accept that museums are spaces where attitude has become form, we must ask whose attitudes and meaning we are referring to and how (and if) we are able to uphold that meaning. The final part of the chapter will introduce the idea of individual curating, an activity that involves rejection as well as selection and revision as well as renewal, acts that are at odds with the accession and deaccession policies of many museums. Engaging with choice and judgement in the construction of a version of ourselves is an activity we take for granted. I will contrast individual curation and agency with the tightly regulated and heavily authored discipline of museum curation where the curatorial eye and curatorial decision-making is institutionally protected. The liberty we have to individually shape and reshape our personal identity seems, for now at least, to be ideologically distanced from the type of collective, visual, national identity that is communicated in collections and shaped by connoisseurs, directors, and influencers from a different time with very different values and ideas.

Chapter 2 is focused on interpretation. When I first joined the staff of Tate, at that point still The Tate Gallery, interpretation was not a familiar term: we had no interpretation curators and no department devoted to this activity. Throughout the 1980s after Nicholas Serota became director, things began to change. Serota came from an exhibition background and had been the director of Whitechapel Gallery and Modern Art Oxford. His ambition for Tate was to reflect a more dynamic attitude to exhibition making and display and create a new visual dialogue.

In a symposium I attended in the late 1980s, I remember Neil MacGregor, Director of the National Gallery expressing pleasure at the way that visitors used the gallery as if they were visiting old friends expecting to find their favourite works of art in familiar locations. Serota on the other hand wanted to shake things up, move work around, change context, present new ideas, and invite new connections. For him, chance, accident, and stumbling across familiar work in an unfamiliar setting, although initially disquieting, would be ultimately rewarding. The introduction of *New Displays*, a total re-hang of the collection, left many visitors feeling confused, they didn't really understand why work had been uprooted and moved. To address this, text in the form of explanation and interpretation was introduced. In this chapter I investigate the authorship, origin, character, and growth of museum interpretation and trace its transformation from its most basic format with the name, birth, and death of artist, date of work, medium and collection number, to a newly expanded caption, wall text and room panel.[1] These newer versions of text were longer and more elaborate with descriptions and explanations that were often embellished with opinion, comment, and direction.

There have been many instances in my working career when the attitude of a director, curator, or high-level administrator has been at odds with visitor expectations. As stated above, one such instance was Serota's desire to inject new life into collection displays with a regular re-hang and a thematic rather than chronological display.[2] Another was the requirement that schoolchildren should have the opportunity of visiting a museum as part of the national curriculum. As laudable as this policy was, museums struggled to cope with an exponential rise of school visits. Many of the children visiting were studying GCSE art or 'A' level art history and had chosen a specific artwork for their final project but when they arrived, (with no internet to help them), the chosen work was out on loan or in conservation. School children travelling from distant locations were dreadfully disappointed and teachers were furious. However plaintively we in the education department begged curators to consult with us if they were planning to remove a work that was popular with students, we were told that schoolchildren were not their priority.

It was also in the 1980s that the issue of free entrance for museums came back on the political agenda. Serota and MacGregor were active campaigners, adamant that UK museums should not only remain free but be physically, socially, and intellectually accessible for all. This was never going to be a 'free lunch' and museums had to prove to government that they were worthy of continued (but as it turned out, reduced) financial support and ensure that exhibitions, displays, events, and activities would appeal to diverse audiences. It was decided that text would provide visitors with the information they needed and explain changes of context. Text would also be used to communicate the museum's mission and strategy and finally, most importantly text would address inclusivity and access by providing increased interpretation. It should be noted however, that there is still very little research into the words that are positioned alongside works of art, how and if they increase understanding or whether they reduce what might once have been a physical, corporeal experience of looking, into a text-driven look and read, check and trace, activity. This chapter will examine and evaluate the ideas and ideology behind interpretative text.

Chapter 3 takes as its central theme, space, place, emplacement, and specifically the way in which museums have reconfigured new spaces to become new sites of meaning. Here, I will use Foucault's concept of heterotopias and suggest that museums are balancing conflicting aspirations to become spaces "in which time never stops building up and topping its own summit" with time "at its most flowing, transitory and precarious".[3] I will propose that Tate Modern's Turbine Hall is a successful example of a physical space that addresses these conflicts of ideological meaning.

Finally, in Chapter 4, I will use Felix Ensslin's, "will to know"[4] to interrogate the expansion of the museum to include new exhibition space, new media space, and new space for interrogation and discourse. I will ask what we mean by the will to know, whose will we are talking about, and in reference to the decolonisation of the museum, what it is was we wanted to know... *then*. I will discuss Eve Tuck and K. Wayne Yang's paper, 'Decolonization is not a metaphor'[5] and examine the position they take and criticism they make of what they perceive to be an all too easy adoption of the decolonising discourse by a range of educational advocacy and scholarship with schools, teaching institutions, libraries, reading lists, and academic writing aligning themselves within the same discourse. With reference to museums, I am keen to examine how the motivation and institutional structure that supports our national collections is rooted in what Tuck and Yang call, *settler/appropriator guilt*. I will suggest that this phrase has never ceased to be relevant for our understanding of how our collections were formed, how they have been curated, and how they are currently retained, explained, and (re)interpreted.

Notes

1 Adrian George, *The Curator's Handbook: Museums, Commercial Galleries, Independent Spaces* (London: Thames and Hudson, 2015), 214.
2 The thematic display was first introduced in Tate Modern but later Tate Britain also adopted this strategy for specific galleries
3 Michel Foucault and Jay Miskowiec "Of Other Spaces" *Diacritics* vol. 16, no. 1 (1986): 22–27.
4 Felix Ensslin "The Subject of Curating – Notes on the Path towards a Cultural Clinic of the Present" *ONCURATING*, no. 26 (October 2015): 20.
5 Eve Tuck and K. Wayne Yang "Decolonization is not a metaphor" *Decolonization: Indigeneity, Education & Society*, vol. 1, no. 1 (2012): 1–40.

1 Collecting, Exhibiting, and Curating

The Permanent Collection

Tony Bennett's seminal book, *The Birth of the Museum*[1] begins with Foucault's proposition that museums are heterotopias of indefinitely accumulating time ... worlds within worlds that represent all time, all epochs, all form, and all taste. Foucault does not confine himself to one definition of the heterotopic space, he also refers to fairgrounds and festivals where time is fleeting and transitory. A juxtaposition of the all-encompassing, eternal, and everlasting with the fleeting, contingent, and transitory reminds me of Baudelaire's definition of modernity, "the ephemeral, the fugitive, the contingent, one half of art, the other being the eternal and the immutable".[2] In this chapter, I want to examine opposing concepts of time within the art museum and how they manifest themselves in different forms of collecting and display: the permanent collection fulfilling Foucault's notion of all time, all epochs, all form and forever, while the temporary exhibition is closer in character to the fairground or festival in its fleeting, transitory, and contingent nature. In addition, particularly over the last 20 years, a third strand of museum curating has emerged and this I am calling individual or social curating. I want to suggest that this new form of selection and display is encouraging a new response, different levels of participation and heightened expectations of the museum.

Cabinets of curiosity or Wunderkammer have often been described as the forerunner to the modern museum. Highly fashionable in the sixteenth, seventeenth, and eighteenth century and popular with wealthy merchants, nobility, naturalists, princes, and academics, they were extraordinarily beautiful, carefully manufactured cabinets, sometimes even whole rooms, designed to show off eclectic objects in the hope that they would provoke wonder and amazement.[3] They also acted as shop fronts or calling cards for wealthy individuals and signifiers of

DOI: 10.4324/9781003213130-2

knowledge, connoisseurship, and taste. On a simple level, collections were a very personal, idiosyncratic amassing of chosen items,[4] predominantly for the collector's pleasure with value taking a secondary role[5] but there were other, undoubtedly more serious motivations like increasing personal status or to borrow from Bourdieu's terminology, gaining additional cultural capital.

Towards the end of the eighteenth century, displaying objects in beautifully crafted cabinets with the intention of provoking amazement and wonder became unfashionable[6] and enlightenment values like order and reason took precedence.[7] The public museum was founded on these ideals and random groups of objects were replaced with clearly assigned, carefully structured displays that encouraged visitors to engage with new ideas and new narratives. In their early formation, museums developed these ideas visually; formal education and learning came later. In fact, eighteenth and early nineteenth-century institutions paid little attention to instruction, "museums were just collections of curiosities … with little guidance for the inexpert".[8] As museums grew in stature, greater emphasis was placed on learning, education, and improving the mind. Grouped with libraries, public lecture halls, and art galleries, they were expected to be, "instruments capable of improving man's inner life".[9] Being inclusive, accessible, and restorative,[10] was highly prized, both then and now and current DCMS policy stresses the crucial contribution that museums make "to the regeneration, health and wellbeing of our regions, cities, towns and villages".[11]

The transition of privately owned, randomly displayed collections, into a more orderly categorisation of work in public museums was largely due to an increase of displayable objects but there were also changes of attitude regarding assessment and value. Institutional, rather than individual judgment became the accepted measure of worth. If a work was acquired by a museum, it was, de facto, valuable. This increased the status and prestige of curators and directors who became powerful, influential taste makers. Jean-Christophe Ammann, whose curatorial journey started at the Kunsthalle under Harald Szeemann, was asked at a Tate conference about the importance of the directors' role. He replied that you should be able to 'smell' him/her as you enter a museum. Chris Dercon, compared his tenure as director of Tate Modern to "taking the helm of a particularly difficult to steer ocean liner",[12] and current director, Maria Balshaw has expressed her intention to make Tate, "the most artistically adventurous and culturally inclusive gallery in the world."[13] The Museum of Modern Art's (MoMA) first director, Alfred Barr went even further, creating an epistemology to shape the way generations of artists, art historians, and art lovers studied modern European and American art.

Many museum directors have become high-profile, high-status influencers, visionaries, and inspirational leaders. They are dedicated to the promotion, development, and status of their institutions. You might say that they are the composers and conductors of a symphony and their curatorial team, principal members of the orchestra.

People are fascinated with the job of the curator even though they often have no idea what it entails. It is a specialist role involving detailed research into the provenance of individual works, in-depth knowledge of an artist or group of artists, a period of art history and art theory. Curators must also be experienced in the display, management, and maintenance of the collection. This is a rather conventional description of the curatorial role. Modern definitions mention other qualities, "the contemporary art curator is no longer an expert on a particular period, instead the curator is an anthropologist, a reporter, a sociologist, an epistemologist, an author, an NGO representative or an observer of the internet".[14] To this alternative list of curatorial attributes, former Tate director, Nicholas Serota adds, "the curator can no longer be seen solely as the dispassionate judge of quality ... the curator is a collaborator, often engaging with the artist to accomplish the work".[15]

Museums with permanent collections are custodians of work that is, by definition, permanently in the collection and must, therefore, be available, either on view or in store, in perpetuity. This is increasingly problematic for directors, academics and curators who question the viability of keeping work in perpetuity. Rosalind Krauss refers to Thomas Krens, director of the Guggenheim, "what was revealed to him was not only the tininess and inadequacy of most museums, but that the encyclopaedic nature of the museum was 'over'".[16] Krens himself said, "the notion of the encyclopaedia only makes sense in a world that is not mobile".[17]

The decision to acquire a work is based on many factors but the trajectory of art history, as it has been, or how it might develop together with the current shape and future form of the collection, will always be a factor. Museums are keen to be open and transparent about their acquisition policy, but the language they use, shows how difficult this can be. MoMA claims to have "a unique point of view that is carefully shaped by its curators, who are always mindful of historical precedents as they look ahead to future developments",[18] Tate speaks of,

> trying to ... form a collection which is both fine in quality and shows the richness and variety of modern art, with representations of all

the major movements and with the greatest artists each represented by several works, or groups of works.[19]

Tate's acquisition policy also refers to, "significant developments in art in all areas covered by the remit ... of outstanding quality, and distinctive in aesthetic character or importance".[20] The phrase, significant developments in art and *aesthetic* character exposes the rather indeterminate nature of acquisition policy.

The word aesthetic is defined as the philosophical study of beauty and taste and used by Kant to expound his theory that aesthetic judgements are inevitably subjective and impossible to support by any interpersonal means, concepts that are problematic for museum curators. There are theorists who believe that aesthetic encounters with artworks are immediate, non-inferential and sensory while others argue that aesthetic judgements are shaped by art history. Prioritising art history over aesthetics or vice versa is the main topic of a group of conversations organised by James Elkins.[21] In the introduction to the series Robert Gero states that, "the aesthetic is a contested space – a multiply defended zone of discourses occupied by theorists working within the disciplines of art history and philosophy".[22] Referring to aesthetics in relation to a museum's collecting policy, presupposes that aesthetics and art history are junctures on the same path, or at the very least deeply connected, "art history without aesthetics is inconceivable ... because art history is first of all constituted by the evidential record of previous aesthetic".[23] Thierry de Duve would agree that art history and aesthetics are inextricably linked, whereas Elkins sees them as totally disconnected, that aesthetics is a means to a nonaesthetic understanding of art history.

If the aesthetic is ever a factor for curators when they make acquisitions, it is rarely mentioned, whereas more practical considerations, like the condition of the work, availability, cost, politics, style, and fashion[24] are always factors. Timing is also critical, if a work suddenly becomes available in auction or is donated as part of a bequest. Gifts are regularly offered and just as often rejected, which is understandable, given that new acquisitions require documentation, cataloguing, and looking after, in perpetuity. Even after a work has entered the collection, it will not automatically, or in some cases, *ever* be displayed. Like many other major art institutions, Tate has a huge body of work in store[25] and the decision to display a work will be influenced by popularity, status, relevance and space (even weight can be a factor).[26]

Documentation relating to the foundation of the museum makes clear that museums "hold work in trust for the nation and the public, not a super serving elite"[27] but as Tate Modern director Frances Morris observes, many collections started out as, "a reflection of the taste, deficiencies, and particular 'hobby horse' passions of directors and curators".[28] Among the small group of collectors who were responsible for the establishment of early UK public art collections, was Sir Henry Tate who donated his collection to the nation, John Julius Angerstein whose 38 paintings of Italian, Dutch, Flemish, and English origin formed the origins of the National Gallery and Sir Hans Sloane, doctor and collector, whose enormous collection became the foundation of the British Museum. Regrettably, all three of these major collectors had links to the slave trade, Angerstein for example, owned a third share in slave estates in Grenada and used profits from the slave trade to build his art collection. In a move towards transparency, some museums are now openly discussing these matters. In a special section of its website called, Tate Galleries and Slavery, Tate includes the following statement, "there can be no doubt that British culture was shaped by the institution of slavery in many, fundamental ways ... we believe the firms founded by the two men which later combined as Tate & Lyle, do connect to slavery".[29]

In the eighteenth century, museums had no written acquisition policy and there were no rules or guidelines to influence decisions made to buy specific works. In 1855, Sir Charles Eastlake travelled through Europe on a vast shopping spree and bought Italian paintings he thought would be worthwhile additions to the National Gallery. These works were predominantly what he liked and what interested him. In other words, it reflected his own taste and that of his Trustees.[30] In many ways this very personal selection process, resembles that of earlier private collectors. Then and now, personal taste has always played an important role in the shaping and development of national collections, and it would be naïve to believe that this is no longer a factor.

The move away from private to public collections signalled a shift of emphasis from the purely enjoyable to the socially serious. Cabinets of curiosity functioned in a playful way, the "poetics and politics of the cabinet of curiosities offer[ed] a form of resistance to the totalising ambitions of reason, a place where the human mind [was able] to play instead of working".[31] In contrast, public museums had more serious ambitions, they were dedicated to inclusiveness, instruction, appreciation, research, and scholarship. They were also spaces where changes in art history and attitudes to art practice were played out.

Modernism and modernist values from the late nineteenth to the mid-twentieth century were rooted in logic, originality, tradition, liberty of expression, and a belief in an abstract truth of life. Postmodernist thinking, from the middle to latter part of the twentieth century was more concerned with the irrational and illogical and favoured a fragmented, eclectic and critical view of previous theoretical positions. How we come to view the present is still being decided. The twenty-first century might be characterised as a digital age, an age of knowledge consumerism or an individualised society, a product of liquid modernity,[32] digital modernity, or identity modernity. Whichever definition we choose, there are indications that we have entered a "new period of transition and epistemological uncertainty".[33]

Marion Endt uses the phrase, *transition and epistemological uncertainty* to support her proposition that "concepts of curiosity and the marvellous resurface at different moments in cultural history".[34] This fits perfectly with the historical period with which this book is concerned, the latter half of the twentieth and beginning of the twenty first-century, a moment in museum history that I would suggest, is exactly *that* ... a moment of transition and epistemological uncertainty, when institutional frameworks of knowledge and meaning are being scrutinised and traditional values and institutional identity, regularly challenged. A moment, too, of doubt in the sustainability and continual expansion of the permanent collection and unease regarding the desirability (or possibility) of material objects becoming *permanent* signifiers of the passing of time.

There are signs too of a conflict of ideology and methodology as curators shape new visual identities that both challenge and/or replace outmoded legacies, and directors, architects, and designers re-imagine the museum space in the hope that this will reconfigure its mission and purpose. It may not be surprising that this period of indeterminacy has given rise to the creation of new identities and an overly enthusiastic appropriation of 'the turn'. The curatorial turn, the deconstructive turn, the ethical turn, post-colonial turn, educational, social, postmodern, and epistemological turn,[35] are all turns that are acting as a discursive frame for the reshaping, re-evaluating and re-centring of collections and the claiming of a space where a repositioning of theory, structure, and the management of museums and revision of theoretical ideas can take place. Museums have been forced to embrace opposing ideologies, showing their allegiance to the maintenance of permanent collections that signify status and nationhood, traditional values, and longevity, while at the same time, welcoming a new form of exhibition making that encourages dissent, discourse, and dialogue. Some might see this as an impossible conflict of objectives, but there are many directors who enthusiastically embrace the symbiotic nature of different ideologies and methodologies as potentially advantageous.

In an interview with Hans Ulrich Obrist, and in answer to the question, are you against the idea of separating collections from exhibitions, Pontus Hultén replied,

> Yes, otherwise the institution has no real foundation ... I think the encounter between the collection and the temporary exhibition is an enriching experience ... a collection isn't a shelter into which to retreat, it's a source of energy for the curator as much as the visitor.[36]

Hultén is expressing his appreciation of the energy and dynamism of the permanent collection as the backbone of an institution.[37] Frances Morris is also a strong believer in the intellectually nourishing role of the permanent collection. In her keynote speech at Museum of Contemporary Art (MCA) in Melbourne in 2016,[38] she referred to the display of different groups of work from different time periods as *a dynamic interplay of concepts and ideas* and described the permanent collection as an interlocuter in dialogue with the contemporary collection. Both Hultén and Morris are keen to draw attention to the very real advantages of museums that house both contemporary and historic collections and even though Morris believes that a museum's permanent collection will always show signs of "inherent contradictions, utopias, dystopias, blind alleys and occasional misguided decision making", she is confident that it will also be "a symbolic and real example of cultural, economic, intellectual and social capital and without it, the museum might become an exhibition space that holds no history and leaves no legacy".[39]

The Temporary Exhibition

The first part of this chapter has looked at the way in which attitudes towards collecting for a permanent collection are focused on notions of longevity and posterity. I will now examine temporary exhibition making and suggest that this form of display is closer in character to the cabinet of curiosity with the curator, taking the role of individual collector.

If Marjatta Hölz is right in her observation that institutions are "increasingly focus[ing] their activity on temporary monographic or thematic exhibitions and events"[40] why might this be so? One hypothesis is that the less permanent nature of a temporary display is an attractive proposition for curators who want to bypass expectations of longevity and timelessness and explore concepts that are more contingent and topical. Shorter, temporary exhibitions act as visual interrogations or conversations that are challenging and disruptive, they

> collect – without suffering the consequences of the obstacles that isolate or disperse works – works of art that when gathered together, acquire a normative value or a programme of reproduction. By mobilizing material and intellectual means, without measures common to permanent exhibitions, they can concretely produce, within a relatively short timeframe, what has been elaborated for countless years in museums and in books on the history and theory of art.[41]

As well as their interventionist nature, as an exclamation mark in the museum narrative, exhibitions are a source of significant income, particularly important for London museums where entrance to the permanent collection is generally free. Taking maximum advantage of this revenue source, museums have begun to expand their annual exhibition programme with more frequent smaller in-focus and monographic artist displays. This new direction has radically changed the working pattern and character of the institution as well as significantly increasing the workload of art handlers who are required to negotiate charts of enormous complexity and work with military style precision on timetables that accommodate frequent changes in both exhibitions and permanent collection displays.

In Judith Masai's essay in *Museums After Modernism*,[42] she states that "there is no such thing as a visitor" with an emphasis on the indefinite article. In other words, it is a mistake to speak of a single visitor or sole visitor type. Similarly, it is impossible to speak about exhibitions in a generic fashion. They are part of the history of an institution, and as such, they may either reflect or challenge its mission, structure, display, and acquisition strategy. An exhibition acts as an intervention, an interrogation and/or a deconstruction of museum philosophy, and often challenges the "allegiance and affinity to the very tradition [it may] seek to displace".[43]

Exhibitions may be arranged according to medium, (paintings, sculpture, photography, installation) or time frame, (decade or century), gender, identity, philosophy, (phenomenology, existentialism, psychoanalysis) or an artists' life. The display might take as its central theme, historical change like a world war or economic disruption, an artistic group with similar interests, like naïve, outsider, or folk art, or a friendship like Picasso and Matisse, Gauguin and Van Gogh, or an 'ism' like modernism, postmodernism, surrealism, minimalism, or pop art. They may also take the form of a grand survey show, an annual competition like the Turner Prize or be cyclical, biennial, or triennial in nature.

In contrast to the criteria used for the selection and display of the permanent collection, planning a temporary exhibition is conceptually and organisationally different. These smaller, shorter displays have a different starting point, different time frame, and different pace. They often speak with more than one voice, which may at times confuse the visitor. Located within the museum and therefore identified with that institution, they may challenge the dominant ideology and present an alternative story or line of enquiry. In this way, they can be part of, but also apart from, the museum's past and present history, they can look forward while they also glance back, be part nostalgic, part futuristic.

Exhibitions start with an idea that is culturally, socially, and artistically conceived, a blank canvas that the curator uses to explore an idea, concept, or theory with "isolated points – stations or landmarks".[44] To gain approval from the exhibition committee, the initial proposal must be supported by a solid rationale and detailed list of desired works with additional information about the condition of individual pieces and any necessary conservation, transportation to and from the exhibition venue, and information about how the work will be installed. Each one of these considerations will have financial implications, and this will be reflected in the final selection. Work that is already in the permanent collection might need to be recontextualised and adapted to suit alternative narratives and create new context.

Curating is always a collaborative affair involving colleagues within the institution or curators from other museums who are familiar with the subject area, experts on a specific artist, group of artists, genre or theme covered by the exhibition. Collaborating with a guest curator will often add another dimension to the overall vision. There are numerous examples of this type of dynamic pairing including the *Intelligence* exhibition at Tate Britain in 2001, co-curated by Virginia Button from Tate and Charles Esche from the Van Abbemuseum, and *Century City*, an exploration of nine cities curated by nine different curators held at Tate Modern in the same year.

Planning an exhibition will begin years in advance with forecasts relating to likely visitor numbers and decisions about which slot in the year will achieve the greatest revenue. Traditionally, autumn is the most desirable time and most likely to bring the greatest income, whereas the summer show gives the institution an opportunity to experiment with artists and themes that might be less popular and more challenging. The pandemic and subsequent downturn in the economic situation may have impact on this type of annual programming and there are already signs that museums may have had to reduce their large-scale exhibitions and introduce shows of shorter duration.

If we borrow from Bourdieu's concept of cultural capital and specifically his proposition that objectified and institutional forms of cultural capital are only available to individuals with required levels of reading competency, parallels might be drawn with the development, consumption, and understanding of images or image literacy. Exhibitions have become "the primary site of exchange in the political economy of art, where signification is constructed and maintained and occasionally deconstructed".[45] Any statement that refers to the construction and deconstruction of signification is important. Signification is relative, it has no permanence or eternal 'truth',

> as long as we can identify something through signification, we have caught the thing in its essence. For Derrida, signification is an endless chain. Just when we think that we have pinned down the thing in question, we realise that what we have caught is simply another signifier.[46]

Understanding, appreciating or interrogating works of art will never be exclusively about style, subject matter, or content, it will always be affected by its mode of acquisition, method of exhibition and display, and the accompanying institutional interpretation.

The curator is the beating heart of the museum, orchestrating a vision and making possible the intellectual development of an idea as well as ensuring 'an afterlife' for the artist, "after the death of an artist their work continues to evolve ... not literally in his work but in our perception of the work".[47] They are the archaeologist, ringmaster, and choreographer, juxtaposing the familiar with the unfamiliar, exploring different methodologies, challenging emerging theories or sometimes, acting as the mouthpiece and spokesperson for the museum and the artist, in which case they, "speak of, and for, the object that he/she has produced".[48] The subject of curating is not "a subject of the master, but neither is it a subject of the university, it is, like the artist himself, or like the analyst, the subject of a praxis".[49] Ensslin's refusal to accept that the subject of curating is either the subject of the master or the subject of the university or cultural institution, is particularly important for the cultural period that this book covers.

If curators are the "institutionalised recognised experts of the artworld establishment",[50] then Hans Ulrich Obrist, who regularly tops the list of the worlds' most powerful artworld experts, is surely its star.

There are many critics who view that the iconic status of star curators as worrying. They believe that curators have become too influential, too powerful, sometimes even competing with the artist. Curators defend their position and explain that they are exercising "procedures of artistic self-organisation and becoming collaborators in an area in which attributions are uncertain, and therefore also more flexible and negotiable".[51] Affording star-like status to curators is not a new phenomenon. Harald Szeemann achieved his notoriety in 1969 in Kunsthalle, Bern when he staged his exhibition *Live in Your Head; When Attitudes Become Form*. This exhibition was startlingly innovative: it interrogated the most radical artistic movements of the 1960, Minimalism, Body Art, Land Art, Earth Works, Arte-Povera, Fluxus, and other conceptual art movements. Even more radically, it chose to emphasise a shift of artistic focus from space as location, to space inside your head. The show achieved iconic status, influenced many young curators and left a remarkable legacy as well as transforming the actual making of an exhibition into an artform, *in its own right*. It treated the museum space as a laboratory rather than a collective memorial[52] and adopted an experimental as well as an experiential methodology. Szeemann rejected the traditional aestheticised showcase previously favoured by curators and created in its place, a form of "spatial choreography",[53] a stage upon which he would choreograph intricate pieces of movement. The exhibition space became an environment where artists could meet, interact, and engage in dialogue and Szeemann acted as facilitator and enabler, "setting the stage for the curatorial assumption of the artist's creative mantle".[54]

Szeemann devoted as much attention to the empty spaces surrounding and between each artwork, as the work itself. He wanted to give art, a "special aura, a breathing space that it would never have again",[55] and create an atmosphere that was expansive, spiritual, and utopian. He was also keen to display relevant supporting material like plans, lists of works, correspondence, evidence of his thinking process, and references to the relationships he had formed with artists and curators. Making transparent the thinking behind an exhibition has since become popular with modern curators. Hans Ulrich Obrist for example often includes archive material, interviews, and memories.

In response to a renewed interest in the nature and status of the temporary exhibition, there has been a notable growth of university and art school degrees that offer "a foundational narrative of curatorial and exhibition studies"[56] and a proliferation of books, articles, and exhibition-related literature.

Exhibitions have their say and pave the way for other curators, sometimes quite literally. In 2013, Jens Hoffman staged a comeback version of the Szeemann show called, *When Attitudes become Form become Attitudes*. This tribute show, showcasing the work of younger artists born after 1970, took place in San Francisco, Detroit and the Venetian Palazzo of the Prado foundation[57] and included a large-scale model of the original exhibition. I like to think of Hoffman acting like a stalker, fan, or gang member in this obsessive act, (interestingly Szeemann said, only tribes survive[58]), an impressionable teenager cramming his bedroom with posters and memorabilia of a favourite film or pop star. Hoffman's exhibition opened with an archive room, representing "the sequel to an episode that tells you what went before"[59] and included information relating to the original exhibition. When asked in a video interview[60] why he thought the original exhibition had become so iconic, Hoffmann replied that this was the first time that Europe had been exposed to conceptual art from the United States. This was true, but in my opinion, of even greater significance, was Szeemann's decision to cast the curator as a free spirit, an inspired partner of the artist. This was an idea that really captured the imagination of the art world.

It is not uncommon for curators to pay tribute to extraordinary exhibitions but not always in such an overt manner. Reesa Greenberg has written extensively about remembering exhibitions, describing them as *replica, riff, and reprise*.[61] The act of remembering is an important concept for any temporary exhibition, as it is in the process of remembering, that the temporary becomes permanent. Hoffmann's acts of resurrection became both a personal homage to Szeemann and a lasting visual legacy which has kept alive the creative concept of the exhibition, as well as continuing to influence institutional attitude and form.

The museum has never been a neutral space, although at times, it may have hoped to present itself as such, "from the inside the museum effaces itself to become an invisible frame for the art or artifacts, it appears merely to house, conserve and exhibit".[62] It has always had a story to tell, ideas to communicate, and a reputation to uphold and these are attitudes that have influenced its function, policy, and identity. Just as the new art history in the latter part of the twentieth century changed from a context-specific, socio-historical discipline to a revision of the hierarchy of art historical values, exhibitions have developed from "merely a staging of the aesthetic projects of their participants"[63] to a "radical redistribution of what seemed solidly preordained moving from transparency to opacity, from the erasure of aesthetic projects to their over-determination".[64]

The museum exhibition has become the art institutions' cabinet of curiosity with the curator, its privileged, powerful, sometimes wayward but always protected, collector. And not just collector, the curator is implicated in the "democratization of the cir-cumscribed professional relations between artists and those who seek to professionally represent it".[65]

In Obrist's words, exhibition making has become, "the medium through which most art becomes known".[66]

Individual Curating as a Social Act

The roots of the verb to curate come from the Latin *curare*, to take care of, so for example, the curate of a church is expected to look after, nurture, and care for the congregation. The focus of this book is curating in the art museum, a job that uses different methodologies to manage different parts of the collection: if a work has already been acquired or is about to enter the permanent collection, the curator will check its provenance and history, arrange conservation, write the catalogue entry, award an accession number, and make plans either for display or removal to store. If the curator is devising and managing a temporary display, which is less concerned with longevity, it will be the central idea, narrative, or philosophical proposition that shapes its development and artworks will be selected to visually explore the broad parameters of that question. Exhibitions may be used as a provocation or critique of assumptions and values held by the institution as well as challenging attitudes to artistic production.

As the official mediator of the institution, the curator is possibly "the most emblematic worker of the cognitive age".[67] They are responsible for communicating the story that the museum wishes to tell and as sanctioned intermediaries, they fulfil the objectives of a range of institutional and professional networks as well as "the interests of larger and more powerful groups and constituencies".[68] The type of recognised groups and constituencies to which Greenberg et al. refer includes directors, trustees, academics, sponsors, donors, government officials, all powerful well-established influencers. But also, more recently, a new group of influencers has emerged, individuals who view the museum as *their* space. The museum visitor may once have been seen as an empty vessel, a passive receiver of information, but this has changed. They are now actively encouraged to take control of their experience, become contributors not just consumers, producers not simply audience members, participants with real rather than symbolic involvement. Above all, they are encouraged to think and act like curators.[69] These changes did not come out of the blue. Throughout history, the public museum has promoted itself as inclusive and accessible but more recently, it has also become an interactive laboratory and working studio rather than a temple of excellence, a space in which curators and visitors engage in collaborative thinking and sharing in the creative process.

It is this move towards co-curating and co-producing that is central to the proposition I am making. I want to draw attention to the rather ambiguous relationship that exists between curating as a profession characterised by power, authority, and authorship, an activity undertaken by museum curators who care for, manage, interpret, and display what, in their view, best represents the story they wish to tell, and the daily acts of selection and display that individuals have become used to, as they construct a personal identity that best suits them, at any particular moment in time. This ambiguity might be described as, "the culture of lifestyle over culture of connoisseurship".[70]

In some parts of the world with high levels of consumption and production (in 2005 the wealthiest 20% of the world accounted for 76.6% of total private consumption), these personal acts of selection have become habitual. People choose the style of dress that appeals to them, their dress, hairstyle, make-up, how they decorate their homes, their lifestyle, leisure activities, and political affiliations. We are told that this form of individual curating is freely available, but as Hans Belting comments, "free access is a fiction",[71] "freedom has a price. No unchallengeable authority exists ... to reassure that identity is a 'good' one".[72]

Lifestyle, knowledge production, politics, and culture are all paraded in front of our curatorial eye, and we piece together a personal identity that matches the vision we have chosen for ourselves. This image may, if we so wish, be communicated to others in the form of a personal narrative, a visual display that makes new links and new connections. Facebook, Instagram, Pinterest, Snapchat, TikTok, and Tumblr are all networks built on content curation. They encourage us to create, share, and publish the most up-to-date version of our everyday selves. An important feature of these acts of individual image making, or what I am calling personal curating, is that they can be regularly changed, edited, adapted, or simply abandoned when new styles emerge, or we become tired of what we perceive to be an old-fashioned or outmoded image. We have become comfortable with the act of constructing and reconstructing ourselves in this way and readily buy into the idea of identity consumerism.

As this book is concerned with attitude that becomes form, I want to question whether the liberty we have, to select, deselect, and reselect our own self-image has given rise to similar expectations of our museums, leading us to imagine that we might have a heightened level of agency and power to influence and change the way we choose, shape, and consume the art that we are told is *ours* and the legacy that we have inherited.

You will see the immediate conflict of interest.

Individual curating welcomes change, revision, and renewal and will happily reject or disrupt what went before. Museum curating operates within strict guidelines, actively resisting any attempt to 'have a good clear out'. In UK museums, deaccession is still rare. Even the word *museum* implies permanence, the International Council of Museums defines it as a permanent institution that exhibits "tangible and intangible heritage of humanity".[73] But this description is problematic. A collection that represents the visual heritage of what once was considered historically and culturally relevant may now seem like an uncomfortable reminder of a time when class, race, gender, colonial attitudes, and political awareness was very different.

As the permanent home of works of art, many of which have, over time, become part of the furniture, our museums find themselves in a difficult position. They are unable to upgrade or re-fashion work that was acquired long ago, they can only move it around or in some cases, store it in the loft (for loft, read museum store). Although moving work around may change the background narrative and encourage new thinking, it is impossible to re-paint visual references or change a visual narrative. The only option open to museums is to reposition and recontextualise, make new connections, create new links, and hope that these acts, and the addition of interpretative text will somehow change the context of what was being communicated *then* to what is acceptable *now*.

There are also problems with our passion for the encyclopaedic collection based on notions of universality. James Rondeau, Art Institute Chicago says,

> I don't actually embrace the word "encyclopedic" when it comes to our museum. I feel that the term isn't scrutinized enough. We're not actually encyclopedic in our collections. We're broad in general, and deep and varied. ... but I worry about the transparency and the honesty around [the word]. Clearly, it suggests a kind of universality that we as museums don't actually deliver.[74]

So, how to square the circle when individual curating is ubiquitous, an act that begins with a vision of ourselves, an opportunity, "to take identities off the shelf, to deliberately pick and choose those elements we like and want"[75] and museum curating, a uniquely specialist profession, steeped in history, tradition, and accepted codes of value and privilege, and for now at least, solidly opposed to the idea of deaccessioning.

Museums work hard to be accessible, inclusive, and welcoming to all. They reject what they describe as the clean slate or empty receptacle model and encourage visitors to bring their own experience, engage, participate, and become active interpreters and co-producers.[76] But this invitation triggers other expectations. In their newly emancipated status, visitors expect a level of empowerment, in which, "physical or symbolic acts of interaction allow them to determine their own social and political reality"[77] and as active producers, they imagine that they have agency to influence the content, shape, and future of the museum. But museums are fiercely protective of their brand, their authorship, their authority and scholarship, and although there may be opportunities for visitors to participate, interact, even sometimes to become co-artist or performer, it is unlikely that the visitor will influence acquisition policy or change the rules of deaccession, they cannot write museum captions or interpretative panels (there have been occasions where visitors are invited to contribute their own interpretation, but only in the form of a temporary intervention) and they cannot decide how, or if, work will be displayed. The conflict of people versus institutional power is constantly being tested not just in museums but also in the realm of public art and statuary.

The case of the Edward Colston statue is an example of how dangerous it is to assume and/or expect consensus regarding the preservation of tangible and intangible heritage. The vast majority of UK statutory was erected between the 1890s and mid-twentieth century, decades that were largely responsible for "the entrenchment of whiteness and the creation of favourable conditions for the memorialisation of slave-holders and colonialists".[78] The question of what is to be done with statues like these will always provoke differing opinions. The UK government has introduced laws that block their removal and are even demanding a policy of 'retain and explain' (so interpretation becomes the dominant method of 'seeing' cultural artefacts). But many people feel uncomfortable with this. They are uneasy about displaying, either on our streets or in our museums, tangible examples of heritage that do not reflect enlightened views regarding colonialism, even if it is explained.

So, it falls upon curators to find ways of re-positioning and revaluing history and heritage in a climate of changing attitude and values. In Liquid Modernity,[79] Zygmunt Bauman refers to a relentless recycle of directionless self-modernisation. If museums, as spaces of modernity, have become ideological sites where acts of modernisation are performed for their own sake, then curation might simply respond to itself and become its own autonomous mode of practice. There is some evidence that this has already happened and modern exhibitions "mark the transformation of the curator from behind-the-scenes aesthetic arbiter to central player".[80]

Inherent within the operational model of the seventeenth century cabinet of curiosity was a clear understanding of the source of power. Objects were the property of the collector, symbolic of his (usually male) wealth and status and intent to impress the visitor/viewer. Any relationship between the two interested partners was well understood. Following this, in the nineteenth century, museums became recognised publicly owned depositaries housing encyclopaedic collections of objects of "perpetual, and indefinite accumulation of time in an immobile place".[81] In these public spaces, visitors were invited to see outstanding works of art, collected *on their behalf*, exhibited and displayed *for them*, with the intention of providing education and enlightenment thinking. In the twenty-first century, museums have a dual mission, they remain dedicated to their role as the preserver of legacy and history while they are also keen to provoke and challenge past attitudes to heritage and cultural worth.

Museums have always been sites of inclusivity and accessibility and the message they now communicate is that anyone can be an artist, that creativity is for all.[82] Visitors are happy to accept this role and to adopt what Zygmunt Bauman calls a postmodern habitat, "governed by consumer desires and choices". They want to upgrade their position from, "back street driver, criticising the route taken and move forward into the driving seat".[83] But transforming the visitor into driver (curator, creator, artist, and performer) brings problems of its own. If we are all artists, then what exactly is the art museum for? Is this "space of performativity and performance" turning visitors into, "participants in a cultural activity that is both a creation of involvement and the manufacture of the necessary distance of critical reflection and self-consciousness?".[84] The modern museum may have become ideologically more sociopolitical and more conceptually framed. It has certainly become a space for interactivity and participation although there are differences of opinion regarding any underlying motivation for this change.

Claire Bishop suggests that visitors think of engagement as emancipation "from a state of alienation induced by the dominant ideological order – be this consumer capitalism, totalitarian socialism or military dictatorship?".[85] Bishop's belief that visitors engage in participatory activities in order to *escape from alienation or isolation* is at odds with the more popular interpretation, that visitors use engagement and interaction to fulfil a deep need for playful interaction. Either, or both, of these interpretations may be applicable but what is undeniable is a dramatic change in the way in which people are using the museum space. They no longer wish to worship at the high altar of culture, they want to challenge the "settled, and uncontroversial position",[86] that culture has, for centuries, held dear. They have different ideas and expectations. They want to broaden their experience and reimagine the museum as an expanded and re-visioned field of sociocultural experimentation, a space for debate and discussion, talks, lectures, conferences, and events, a space that is physically, socially, intellectually, and culturally accessible,[87] a haven for "convivial community".[88] The museum visitor wants to engage in real collaborative creativity and achieve, "a more positive and non-hierarchical social model".[89]

Although this non-hierarchical social model may not always be evident in the structure, governance, ethnicity, and gender of museum personnel, it is certainly present, in the newly designed physical spaces that offer an environment that is inclusive, accessible, and participative as opposed to what has historically been an elitist, didactic environment. The museum has become an alternative space, a place for interaction and immersive activity, a physical embodiment of Foucault's heterotopia.

And as well as the provision of new spaces, museums have extended opening hours, introduced inclusive and accessible programming, and devised a range of interactive activities to suit the changing demands and lifestyle of its visitors. All great news ... but not without substantial financial challenges. Museums must achieve (and more importantly, sustain) a level of income that facilitates the upkeep of their buildings, maintains excellent standards of conservation, ambitious exhibition programming, and excellent standards of display. It only takes one unexpected event like the recent pandemic or fears of an economic recession to disrupt their smooth running. During the pandemic, museums were forced to close their doors for months, radically depleting their financial reserves and changing (maybe forever), the behaviour of visitors who, unable to visit in person, turned (yet another 'turn') to virtual platforms and online resources.[90]

Time, events, politics, and the environment, as well as people and ideas are central to the formation of history and what we choose as representative of our cultural heritage is exactly that ... *our* choice. Nineteenth-century museums were preoccupied with themes of ever accumulating time and the expansion of encyclopaedic collections, twentieth-century museums placed more emphasis on discussion, debate, and critical discourse, and we can only imagine what central theme will dominate the museum in the twenty-first century.

Our attitudes towards legacy, heritage, and modernism are out of sync. Our public spaces are concrete reminders of the way in which heroes of the past have become antagonists of the present, impossible to depose, so solidly are they rooted in our historical memory. Our permanent collections are struggling to reflect new attitudes relating to authorship, ownership, and value, and exhibitions, as sites of activism where tradition is scrutinised and values reassessed, are keen to present an alternative ideology. If individual curating is influenced by and reflected in the major philosophical concerns of the twenty-first century, and identity, change, and renewal are the current central themes, questions must be asked as to how and if we are able to inject ideas of identity, change, and renewal into our permanent collections or whether these new ideas will seek refuge in a new separate space, a new heterotopia, a new world within a world.

Notes

1 Tony Bennett, *The Birth of the Museum: History, Theory, Politics* (London: Routledge, 1995), 1.
2 Charles Baudelaire, *The Painter of Modern Life and Other Essays*, 2nd ed. trans. Jonathan Mayne (London: Phaidon, 1995), 13.
3 "Stephen Greenblatt suggests that museums encourage two kinds of response: resonance and wonder. 'By wonder,' he writes, 'I mean the power of the displayed object to stop the viewer in his or her tracks, to convey an arresting sense of uniqueness, to evoke an exalted attention.'" Steven Lubar, "Cabinets of Curiosity", *Medium.com*, 1 October 2018 https://lubar.medium.com/cabinets-of-curiosity-a134f65c115a
4 Alma S. Wittlin, *The Museum: Its History and Its Tasks in Education* (London: Routledge & Kegan Paul, 1949), 20.
5 Ibid. Wittlin comments that "the actual material value of collections is likely to be inferior to the impression of wealth they evoke", 23.
6 Although words like these are still used by artists of all disciplines. Hans Ulrich Obrist recalls that Diagilev and Cocteau tried to explain what they did with the words "Etonnez moi!". Interviewing Hans Ulrich Obrist by Tino Monetti (unpublished) https://medium.com/@tinomonetti/interviewing-hans-ulrich-obrist-eng-482b5886abe8
7 Bennett, *The Birth of the Museum*, quotes Greenwood (1888) who asserts that "order and system is coming out of chaos".
8 Alma S. Wittlin, *Museums: In Search of a Usable Future* (Cambridge: MIT Press, 1970), 132.
9 Bennett, *The Birth of the Museum*, 18.

10 It should be noted that using The British Museum as an example, 'accessible' in the early years of the public museum, is not how we might now understand the term. In those early years, those who wished to visit were required to give their credentials in person at an office and then wait about 14 days until they were allowed entry.
11 United Kingdom, Department for Culture, Media and Sport, The Culture White Paper, Cm 9218 (London: HMSO, 2016) accessed 5 November 2022, https://assets.publishing.service.gov.uk/government/uploads/system/uploads/attachment_data/file/510798/DCMS_The_Culture_White_Paper__3_.pdf, 9.
12 Elizabeth Fullerton "Tate Director Chris Dercon: 'Everything can be changed'", *ARTnews*, 27 February 2013.
13 Tate, "Maria Balshaw appointed new director of Tate", press release, 17 January 2017, www.tate.org.uk/press/press-releases/maria-balshaw-appointed-new-director-tate.
14 Heinz Bude, "The curator as meta-artist: The case of HUO", *Texte zur Kunst* 86 (2012): 114.
15 Nicholas Serota, *Experience or Interpretation: The Dilemma of Museums of Modern Art* (London: Thames & Hudson, 2000), 36.
16 Thomas Krens cited in Rosalind Krauss, "The Cultural Logic of the Late Capitalist Museum", *October* 54 (1990): 7.
17 Serota, *Experience or Interpretation*, 36.
18 Inside/Out @ in Context: Criteria for an acquisition www.moma.org/explore/inside_out/tag/acquisition/
19 Nicholas Serota, *Experience or Interpretation*, 11.
20 Tate, *Tate Acquisition and Disposal Policy. Approved by the Board of Trustees on 18 November 2020* (2020) www.tate.org.uk/documents/1685/acquisition_and_disposal_policy_2020.pdf
21 James Elkins, ed., *Art History versus Aesthetics* (New York: Routledge, 2006).
22 Robert Gero, "The Border of the Aesthetic" in *Art History versus Aesthetics*, ed. James Elkins (New York: Routledge, 2006), 3.
23 Ibid.; Thierry de Duve in *Art History versus Aesthetics*, ed. James Elkins (New York: Routledge, 2006), 60.
24 "All decisions regarding acquisitions take into account the needs of the Collection, the condition of the work and costs of conserving and storing the work; the potential for display at relevant Tate site(s); and that any purchase has been negotiated to represent the best possible price to Tate." Tate, *Tate Acquisition and Disposal Policy*, 2020, www.tate.org.uk/documents/1685/acquisition_and_disposal_policy_2020.pdf
25 Marjatte Hölz, "Fresh Breeze in the Depots — Curatorial Concepts for Reinterpreting Collections", *OnCurating* no. 12 (2011): 2. In this article Hölz observes that 'much of museums' collections are kept in store without ever being shown for various reasons (qualitative, conservational, financial, spatial, etc.).
26 Edward Mayer, Head of Gallery Management for Tate recalls that the original American architect of Tate Britain's Duveen gallery designed the

26 *Collecting, Exhibiting, and Curating*

     space so that statues arranged in two rows either side of the centre would stand on reinforced parts of the floor.
27 Frances Morris, "Expanding horizons: rethinking the past through the lens of the present" (Keynote speech at the Museum of Contemporary Art, Melbourne, Australia, 2016), https://youtu.be/UrCyyt5z1Ow. In her speech Morris quotes from Boris Groys who described the traditional museum as a place of things and the contemporary museum as a space of events.
28 Ibid.
29 "The Tate galleries and slavery", Tate, accessed 4 November 2022, www.tate.org.uk/about-us/history-tate/tate-galleries-and-slavery
30 Art for the Nation: Sir Charles Eastlake at the National Gallery, www.nationalgallery.org.uk/about-us/history/directors/sir-charles-lock-eastlake
31 Peter Mason, "The Song of the Sloth" in *Re-verberations, Tactics of Resistance, Forms of Agency in Trans/cultural Practices*, ed. Jean Fisher (Maastricht: Jan van Eyck, 2000), 28.
32 Zygmunt Bauman, *Liquid Modernity* (Cambridge: Polity, 2000).
33 Marion Endt, *Reopening the Cabinet of Curiosities: Nature and the Marvellous in Surrealism and Contemporary Art* (PhD diss., University of Manchester, 2008), 3.
34 Ibid.
35 Rachel Esner and Fieke Konijn, "Curating the Collection: Editorial", *Stedelijk Studies* 5 (2017), https://stedelijkstudies.com/journal/curating-the-collection/
36 Hans Ulrich Obrist, *A Brief History of Curating* (Zürich: JRP Ringier, 2011), 47.
37 Ibid.
38 Morris, *Expanding Horizons: Rethinking the Past through the Lens of the Present"*. In this speech, Morris outlined her vision for redefining the museum for the 21st century.
39 Ibid.
40 Hölz, "Fresh Breeze in the Depots", 2.
41 Jean-Marc Poinsot, "Large Exhibitions: A Sketch of a Typology" in *Thinking about* Exhibitions, eds. Reesa Greenberg, Bruce W. Ferguson, and Sandy Nairne (London: Routledge, 1996), 40.
42 Judith Mastai, "There Is No Such Thing as a Visitor" in *Museums after Modernism: Strategies of Engagement, New Interventions in Art History*, eds. Griselda Pollock and Joyce Zemans (Oxford: Blackwell, 2007), 173–178.
43 Okwui Enwezor, "The Postcolonial Constellation: Contemporary Art in a State of Permanent Transition" in *Antinomies of Art and Culture: Modernity, Postmodernity, Contemporaneity*, eds. Terry Smith, Okwui Enwezor, and Nancy Condee (Durham, Duke University Press, 2008), 211.
44 Reesa Greenberg, "'Remembering exhibitions': From point to line to web" *Tate Papers* 12 (2009), www.tate.org.uk/research/tate-papers/12/remembering-exhibitions-from-point-to-line-to-web
45 Reesa Greenberg, Bruce W. Ferguson, and Sandy Nairne, eds. *Thinking about Exhibitions* (London: Routledge, 1996), 1.

46 Brian Grassom, "Measure and Excess" in *Analecta Husserliana: The Yearbook of Phenomenological Research* ed. Anna-Teresa Tymieniecka (Cham: Springer, 2007): 160.
47 Caroline Elbaor, "Rem Koolhaas moonlights as co-curator of Milan Exhibition highlighting Sol LeWitt's links to architecture", Artnet News, 15 November 2017, https://news.artnet.com/art-world/sol-lewitt-rem-koolhaas-curator-1148495
48 Felix Vogel, "Notes on Exhibition History in Curatorial Discourse", *OnCurating* no. 21 (2013): 48.
49 Felix Ensslin, "The Subject of Curating – Notes on the Path towards a Cultural Clinic of the Present", *OnCurating* no. 26 (2015): 28.
50 Mari Carmen Ramirez, "Brokering Identities: Art Curators and the Politics of Cultural Representation" in *Thinking about Exhibitions* eds. Reesa Greenberg, Bruce Ferguson, and Sandy Nairne (London: Routledge, 1996), 22.
51 Dorothee Richter, "Artists and Curators as Authors – Competitors, Collaborators, or Team-workers?" *OnCurating* no. 19 (2013): 43.
52 Obrist, *A Brief History of Curating*, 83.
53 Teresa Gleadowe, "Introduction" in *Exhibiting the New Art: 'Op Losse Schroeven' and 'When Attitudes Become Form'*, 1969 (London: Afterall, 2010), mentions Christian Rattemeyer's deep interest in spatial choreography, 11.
54 Ibid.
55 Melanie Tran, "Harald Szeeman's 'Project Files'", *Getty Research Institute: Outside the Box* (blog), 31 May 2013, https://blogs.getty.edu/iris/treasures-from-the-vault-harald-szeemanns-project-files/
56 Nanne Burmann and Dorothee Richter, "Editorial: Documenta: Curating the History of the Present" *OnCurating* no. 33 (2017): 2.
57 Jens Hoffmann, *Show Time: The Most Influential Exhibitions of Contemporary Art* (London: Thames & Hudson, 2017), 186.
58 Quote from Una Szeemann in "A closer look: Being Harald Szeemann" www.youtube.com/watch?v=Vu6zn-V11vI
59 Museum of Contemporary Art Detroit, "Jens Hoffman interview: 'When attitudes became form become attitudes'", 12 February 2013, video, 3:33, https://youtu.be/3JwXvOrxK5o
60 In conversation with artist Carey Young at a Tate event, Jens Hoffman discussed 'a canon of curating'. This was a critical discussion that considered questions around the role of a curator, the major changes that have influenced curating and its relationship to art, artists, and the wider world. "Show time: Curating contemporary art", Tate, accessed 4 November 2022, www.tate.org.uk/audio/show-time-curating-contemporary-art.
61 Greenberg, "Remembering exhibitions".
62 Suzanne Oberhardt quoted in Griselda Pollock, "Un-Framing the Modern: Critical Space/Public Possibility" in *Museums after Modernism: Strategies of Engagement, New Interventions in Art History*, eds. Griselda Pollock and Joyce Zemans (Oxford: Blackwell, 2007), 2.

63 Jean-Marc Poinsot, "Large exhibitions", 39.
64 Ibid., 40.
65 John Roberts quoted in Michael Birchall, "Editorial" *OnCurating* no. 19 (2013): 4.
66 Obrist, *A Brief History of Curating*, 7.
67 Carolyn Christov-Bakargiev quoted in David Balzer, *Curationism: How Curating Took over the Art World and Everything Else* (London: Pluto Press, 2015), 3.
68 Ramirez, "Brokering Identities", 22.
69 See Graham Black on this topic, "Meeting the Audience Challenge in the 'Age of Participation'", *Museum Management and Curatorship* vol. 33, no. 4 (2018): 302–319, https://doi.org/10.1080/09647775.2018.469097
70 Hans Belting, "Contemporary Art as Global Art" in *The Global Art World: Audiences, Markets, and Museums*, eds. Hans Belting and Andrea Buddensieg (Ostfildern: Hatje Cantz, 2009), 38–70.
71 Ibid., 40.
72 Dennis Smith, *Zygmunt Bauman: Prophet of Postmodernity* (Cambridge: Polity, 1999), 107.
73 "A museum is a non-profit, permanent institution in the service of society and its development, open to the public, which acquires, conserves, researches, communicates and exhibits the tangible and intangible heritage of humanity and its environment for the purposes of education, study and enjoyment." International Council of Museums, *Museum Definition*, August 24, 2022, https://icom.museum/en/resources/standards-guidelines/museum-definition/, accessed 4 November 2022.
74 See James Rondeau quoted in Andrew Goldstein, "Museums are contested sites. The Art Institute of Chicago's James Rondeau on why he finds the current moment so electrifying," Artnet News, 23 July 2019, https://news.artnet.com/the-big-interview/james-rondeau-art-institute-of-chicago-interview-part-1-1607410
75 Michael Bhaskar, *Curation: The Power of Selection in a World of Excess* (London: Piatkus, 2016), 285.
76 Tony Butler director of Derby museums has invited young people to act as co-curators and develop a programme of interpretation around Joseph Wright of Derby's life, his family, and wellbeing.
77 Sue Bell Yank, "The role of social art according to Bishop and Mouffe", 20 November 2009, https://suebellyank.com/2009/09/the-role-of-social-art-according-to-bishop-and-mouffe/
78 Peter Hill, "When the statues went up", *History Workshop*, 12 June 2020, www.historyworkshop.org.uk/when-the-statues-went-up/
79 Bauman, *Liquid Modernity*.
80 Ramirez, "Brokering Identities", 21.
81 These ideas are expressed in Foucault and Miskowiec, "Of Other Spaces".
82 Adam Reed Rozan, Director of Audience Engagement, Worcester Art Museum states that museum projects "need to be as much about the audience as they do the objects". "Audience engagement: How museums

Collecting, Exhibiting, and Curating 29

learned to love their visitors", *Museum-iD*, July 2016, https://museum-id.com/audience-engagement-how-museums-learned-to-love-their-visitors-by-adam-rozan/
83 Smith, *Zygmunt Bauman: Prophet of Postmodernity*, 107.
84 Pollock, "Un-framing the Modern", 30.
85 Claire Bishop, *Artificial Hells: Participatory Art and the Politics of Spectatorship* (London: Verso, 2012), 275.
86 Orian Brook, Dave O'Brien, and Mark Taylor, *Culture Is Bad for You: Inequality in the Cultural and Creative Industries* (Manchester: Manchester University Press, 2020), 31.
87 The Nina Simon TED Talk, "The Art of Relevance" offers an excellent discussion on the relevance of art and culture. Nina Simon, "The Art of Relevance" (recorded at TedX, Palo Alto, 2 April 2018), www.youtube.com/watch?v=NTih-l739w4
88 Katie Schick, "The Broken Middle" in *Gillian Rose: A Good Enough Justice*, (Edinburgh: Edinburgh University Press, 2012), 36–54, www.jstor.org/stable/10.3366/j.ctt3fgtr2.6
89 Sue Bell Yank, "The Role of Social Art According to Bishop and Mouffe".
90 The DCMS published a policy document in 2019 that referred to "the Digital Culture Project and the #CultureisDigital. This was an exploration of how culture and technology can work together to drive audience engagement, boost the capability of cultural organisations and unleash the creative potential of technology", United Kingdom, Department for Digital, Culture, Media and Sport, *Policy Paper: Culture is Digital*, updated 18 September 2019, www.gov.uk/government/publications/culture-is-digital/culture-is-digital

2 Interpretation and Text

In Chapter 1, I considered the motivation for displaying objects in seventeenth-century cabinets of curiosity and suggested that ideas comparable to *a showing of the marvellous* are re-emerging in temporary exhibition making. I then turned my attention to the foundation of the nineteenth-century public museum with its emphasis on encyclopaedic collections and notions of tradition, heritage, and legacy, and asked whether a continuing expansion of the permanent collection is viable or even desirable. I now want to move away from collections and display and look specifically at interpretative text and ask why this relatively new addition to the museum experience has become an essential 'add-on' for many visitors.

Text is the museum's rubber stamp of meaning. What used to be a brief couple of lines with basic information, the artists name, date of birth, title, medium, date, and provenance, has undergone a transformation and re-emerged as lengthy authoritative opinion, a written directive on ways of seeing. Protected by institutional authority and supported by a surety of meaning, words that sit alongside works of art seem to defy contradiction and resist any difference of opinion. They are apparently *how the museum sees it*. The premise is that these words are neutral, that they have no agenda. But text is never neutral, it is authored and owned and Edward Said's questions, "who writes, for whom is the writing being done and in what circumstances"[1] is apposite. Similar questions might be asked of museum interpretation, who writes museum text; under what circumstances is it constructed, using which theory, and on behalf of which group of people.

When I first joined Tate in 1987, the word interpretation was rarely used, we had no dedicated department and there were no curators responsible for its production. As we moved towards the end of the century, museum text became demonstrably more present. Pragmatic as well as practical reasons were responsible for its growth, most notably

DOI: 10.4324/9781003213130-3

the decision (initially at Tate Modern but also later at Tate Britain), to display the collection thematically rather than chronologically. Before Serota took over as director in 1988, time-based chronology had been Tate's preferred display methodology and visitors had become used to seeing work in familiar locations. But Serota was keen to challenge what had gone before, destabilise the status quo, move paintings around, choose new locations and create new context. Branded simply, *New Displays* and sponsored by BP (attitudes towards sponsors like BP, Sackler, and others were very different in the 1980s), Tate embarked on an annual re-hang. It was hoped that this shake-up would modernise its image with revitalised branding and marketing, attract new visitors, increase public awareness, and show more of the collection.[2] But Serota also had other more serious motivations. He wanted to redefine the conventions of the permanent galleries, reject the canon of official art history, and challenge accepted paradigms. You could say (and this would fit with Bourdieu's theory on 'field') that Serota was a perfect example of a powerful individual reconstituting a field and imbuing it with new meaning.[3] Dennis Stevenson, Chair of the Trustees at the time of the re-hang commented, "the first re-hang was extraordinarily controversial, but it was clearly strategically correct. The audience doubled. You don't go back to the cinema to see the same film every week, and it's the same with paintings".[4] Later when Chris Dercon became director of Tate Modern, he quoted from Richard Tuttle, "once the order has been found, everything can be changed around' and he continued to use the phrase 'mixing everything around'"[5] as his mantra.

Expecting to see work in different locations using different configurations is now an accepted part of the museum experience but back in the 1980s, regular re-hangs were less common and not entirely welcome. A type of Kraussian narrative trajectory where each room is historically linked to the one before and the one after and organised with obvious and apparent sequentially[6] was replaced with smaller displays showing work from across the twentieth and twenty-first centuries. These rooms had rather obscure titles like *Joie de Vivre*, *Myth and Nature*, *Savage Beauty*, *Existence and Expression*. Choosing a thematic display was a liberating move for Tate and it used this new-found freedom to disrupt the logic of chronology and challenge what had historically been accepted as the evolutionary progress of art history. Inevitably, there were differences of opinion regarding the success of the thematic arrangement with some critics describing it as "an aversion to chronology ... spreading widely and rapidly like an epidemic".[7] In contrast, colleagues and other museum professionals generally judged the new hang with its preference for thematic displays and challenging titles, to be conceptually innovative. Unfortunately, it was the very people who needed help to understand these new configurations (museum visitors) who found it most confusing. In an attempt, to make more transparent institutional decisions that were behind these changes and help visitors better understand the thinking behind *New Displays*, Tate introduced explanatory wall texts and room panels. However, the introduction of more text brought its own problems, and it was not uncommon to encounter large clusters of people at the entrances of exhibitions and displays faithfully reading extended wall panels and then walking rather quickly through the galleries almost as if they were negotiating chapters of a walk-in illustrated book. It was this pattern of behaviour that led many to question whether the museum experience had become primarily "one of saying rather than seeing".[8] Reading institutional text certainly seemed to have become normalised and was often described by visitors as essential for their understanding.

Within Tate, the decision to set up a dedicated department for the writing of text also signalled an important shift of institutional attitude. The appointment of one single curator as official custodian and spokesperson who would write and edit captions and wall texts, produce "an interpretation strategy and conduct a complete overhaul of the production and editing processes",[9] changed the character of the discipline, elevated its status, and gave it new purpose. Tate's first interpretation curator had been a staff member for over twenty-five years, he was familiar with the institution, its history, values, and structure and this made the question, who writes even more important. Simon Wilson[10] stated that he saw his role as, "defender of the general public".[11] He claimed that text was democratising and enabling, but I saw things differently. I found it hard to reconcile Tate's commitment to the provision of multiple interpretations, multiple pathways for understanding, plurality of meaning, and diversity of opinion with the emergence of wall texts and interpretation panels that were written with institutional authority and a strict consistency of style, voice, and tone.

In fact, problems with the perception of institutional text, before the introduction of a department dedicated to the discipline, showed how conflicted this topic had become. Text had no fixed identity, no set position or agreed location. Initially regarded as academic, then journalistic, then educational and finally interpretative, it moved from department to department. Historically, it was the curator who would research, catalogue, establish the provenance, and write the accompanying label for work that was to be displayed. But as the public appetite for written resources grew and it became necessary to produce more leaflets, guides, broadsheets, and catalogues, museum text adopted a journalistic style and moved into the communication department. Much later education staff took over the task, but this was not welcome by everyone. Questions were asked about their academic credentials, were they qualified to write captions and wall texts, did they have the experience and research background or was this the first step in the dumbing down of the museum. Those working in the learning team were confident that an increase in the provision of interpretative text was essential if the museum was to appear inclusive and accessible, but curators were not in favour of longer wall panels, in fact any expansion of the basic label was vehemently opposed. These differences of opinion were not inconsequential. They were symptomatic of interdepartmental and epistemological uncertainty and a significant conflict of interest regarding the importance and status of museum text.

My own research into the growth of interpretation began in the latter part of the twentieth century. I had expected to find a dedicated manual for writing this specialist text, but I soon realised that there was no theory, no literary guidelines, no "specific laws, structures and devices that could be studied in themselves rather than reduced to something else".[12] There was however plenty of information about the practicalities involved, the length, tone, and readability of captions and labels. The optimum length was deemed to be around one hundred words. Sentences were required to be short and simple, and express only one idea, what Beverley Sorrell called, the Big Idea,[13] references to other work might be included, but only if this was in the same room and specialist terminology was to be avoided or at the very least, explained. These guidelines were described by Tate's interpretation editor as "the primary level in a continuum of interpretation"[14] but most visitors viewed institutional text (mainly unauthored although later the name of the curator was included) as more than just the first step, but the *only* step and fundamental to their overall understanding.

Much consideration was given to how visitors would physically encounter wall texts and captions, whether the text was positioned to the left or right of the work, the font style, size, colour, and background of the label. It was likely that any reading would take place 'on the move', in a crowded situation and the brevity of the encounter (data has shown that the first-glance attention span of a visitor is only a few seconds), would influence its content, form and character with "uncomplicated, and immediately engaging"[15] cited as a top priority.

Many books have been written on the most effective form of museum text but, like language, its function will never be one dimensional and the chosen format can never be uniform. In fact, the museum label is unique in character and function. It is not a marketing or promotional tool (although it might sometimes be used for this purpose) or a standard academic document; it is not an extract from a novel or a poem (although elements of these sources might be included) or an advert written to persuade with repeated words and complex grammar (although again sometimes, this might be a feature of interpretative text); it is not a note or a letter communicating a personal message, it is not a recipe to instruct, a pamphlet to inform, or a written explanation of a diagram or chart. Interpretative text offers a verbal explanation of a visual image or object using words that describe how it looks, what it means, how it was made, and the context of its production. Institutions have high expectations of the benefits that this form of text can offer. They claim that it equitably values the visitor, the art object, and the organisational mission, that it addresses inclusivity by encouraging audiences of different backgrounds and knowledge to connect with their own lived experience. It would be hard to argue with any of these ambitions but finding evidence to support claims of this kind, is more difficult to find.

Said also asked, "for whom text might be written". With reference to the museum, the answer to this question must surely be the visitor and visitors are very complimentary. They frequently say that 'they love having it' and rely on it being there. When pressed to say exactly what it is that text gives them over and above looking at the image, they regularly mention context, meaning and artistic intention.[16] I want to consider all three of these in more detail, beginning with context.

In relation to context, Norman Bryson observes, this "apparently straightforward concept belies a range of assumptions, many of which are rarely interrogated or openly exposed".[17] I want to consider the relationship of context and text and suggest that even though the two words are both nouns, context has the feel of an adjective, working for text, actively helping visitors see better, or more deeply. Visitors have high expectations of the additional meaning that any text based information will provide but where does this leave the actual artwork or as Bryson calls it, the visual text? Is it passive, simply an illustration of the text, does it in fact assume the responsibility of a text "waiting for the context to come to order its uncertainties and determinations".[18] Is Matisse right in his observation that, "many people like to think of painting as an appendage of literature and therefore want it to express, not general ideas suited to pictorial means, but specifically literary ideas".[19] Bryson suggests that context and text are predestined antonyms, that the two are working against one another (he does, in fact, speak of implied opposition), that in its role as explanatory agent for text, context occupies a position of enhanced status and subsequently takes control. If context does in fact control text, then museum interpretation, as context, cannot be thought of as simply additional, instead, it becomes the dominant means by which gallery visitors construct meaning. Museums are confident that context gives visitors, a way in, but it is also possible that it provides them with a way out, a substitute for looking, a prop or diversion. In her reference to "representation hover[ing] on the edge between these two, incommensurable yet inextricable means",[20] Mieke Bal uses the words, *about and for*. Context may help a visitor look in, but it might also divert attention and problematise the immediate encounter.

As well as context, museum visitors suggest that knowledge of artistic intention is critical for their understanding. However, this presupposes that an artist is able (or has the desire) to fix the intention and meaning of a work. In one of many interviews with David Sylvester, Francis Bacon said,

> suddenly the lines that I'd drawn suggested something totally different, and out of this suggestion arose this picture. I had no intention to do this picture; I never thought of it in that way. It was like one continuous accident mounting on top of another.[21]

In this quote Bacon is emphasising the importance of serendipity, surprise, loss of control, and an acceptance of the unexpected. In contrast, museum text, if it is to fulfil its institutional remit, chooses words that are assured, assertive, and controlled. Theorists who believe in absolute intentionalism, are confident that "a work's meaning and artistic intention are logically equivalent".[22] If this is true, then the kind of interpretation that visitors crave, might not have a role to play, but as Danto says,

> because of the essential ambiguity of the relationship between production and reception, every representation, every sign, is potentially open to interpretation, open to being taken as a witness both to what may and to what may not have been intended and whose effectiveness is also largely a function of time, place, and circumstance.[23]

Notwithstanding questions like these, establishing meaning is equally important for visitors and art historians alike, "why was it so pressing for Alfred Barr to establish the painting's ultimate meaning? My hypothesis is that it was mostly to pacify it".[24]

The desire to pacify and control may also be described as a struggle of presence over meaning,

> In a rush to make sense of the circumstances in which we find ourselves, our tendency in the past was to ignore and forget "presence" in favour of "meaning". Interpretations were hurled at objects in order to tame them, to bring them under control by endowing them with meanings they did not necessarily possess.[25]

Moxley refers to interpretation being hurled at objects to tame them and bring them under control. He suggests that meaning will always be new meaning that they (the paintings) did not necessarily possess. This idea is critical for interpretation, "the more arguments deployed to show that the correct interpretation of the image has been reached—the most well documented and solidly grounded—the less chance there will be for the image to grow unruly. I have always been a fan of the 'unruly'",[26] I believe that curiosity and unrest are an important part of the museum experience and that leaving a gallery feeling challenged and puzzled is a sign of real engagement. Without uncertainty, the visit becomes an exercise in learning rather than an unsettling, journey of exploration and potential discovery.

Museum text is not a line of words releasing a single 'theological' message of the Author-God, but a contribution to a multidimensional space in which a variety of writings, none of them original, blend and clash.[27] Our museums are full of interpretative texts, many of which were written years ago. What we hear when we read these texts will not be the same as what might have been 'heard' when the text first appeared. This is important. As Barthes says, "we do not know who is speaking; the text speaks that is all".[28] So given that our permanent collections reflect a time in which attitudes were very different, we need to ask whether this text is a new translation, a reinterpretation or a re-evaluation of the original message. According to Paul Ricœur, "the very work of interpretation reveals a profound intention, that of overcoming distance and cultural differences and of matching the reader to a text which has become foreign".[29]

Curators 'share interpretative strategies' for constituting artistic properties and assigning artistic intentions and this knowledge is communicated as institutional interpretation. But unless we believe in absolute intentionalism, any meaning inevitably becomes new meaning, new information, new knowledge. In this sense, the curator becomes a newsreader. Newsreaders play a double game, they introduce their own interpretive strategy while reading someone else's text and rely on communal norms when communicating the methods and results of this interpretation to their reader.[30] It might be said that the curator, educator, or interpreter plays a similar double game, they are also double agents. As newsreaders, they 'read' the visual text, (the painting), invariably with reference to other texts which may be written or visual and then communicate an updated version back to the visitor, in what they assume to be a form of language that is accessible and easily understood. Curators are involved in, "a double operation of advance and containment ... [in an act which] liberates with one hand [and] legislates with the other".[31]

In *Über Sinn und Bedeuting* [*Sense and Reference*], Gottlob Frege, talks about the 'what' of discourse as opposed to the 'what about'.[32] The what, as sense, correlates the identification and predicative function within a sentence, the what about, its reference, or how it relates to the world. Frege also refers to deep and superficial encounters, "if we call an observation deep, we praise it for giving new and more complex meaning. A superficial encounter might be lacking these qualities, unable to go beyond or under, the first impression produced by the phenomenon in question".[33] If deep, in the sense that Gumbrecht uses it, is similar in feel to going under or beyond one's first impressions, this might fulfil a central aim of written interpretation, that it will offer the visitor a more meaningful way of understanding a work of art (and visitors seem hopeful that museum text *will* facilitate a deeper encounter, improve their experience, and provide full or fuller meaning) but whether attaining full or fuller meaning is possible, necessary, or even desirable is yet to be agreed and even if it is possible to find a deeper truth that resides outside of the object, this may radically change the relationship of what is said of the thing, to the thing itself, that which it seeks to contextualise or elaborate. In addition, even if interpretative text (content, context, intention, and meaning), has the ability to go beyond, to extend and expand knowledge of the visual, how and where will that new knowledge be communicated? Text may need to find another, different, separate space, distanced and disconnected from the visual text and in this new conceptual space, it may find itself apart from rather than *a part of* the source of its focus.[34] Similarly, if interpretation provides the *what about*, for the what of an artwork, it too, may be forced into another space, alienated from the visual text to which it owes its very being.

Some theorists believe that meaning and presence are antonyms. They warn that meaning might take priority over presence and in certain situations become the dominant form of understanding. Others believe that it is possible for them to coexist,

> within this specific constellation, meaning will not bracket, will not make the presence effects disappear, and the—unbracketed—physical presence of things (of a text, of a voice, of a canvas with colours, of a play performed by a team) will not ultimately repress the meaning dimension.[35]

The opposing views that Gumbrecht and Moxley express are important. If Moxley is correct and the type of meaning museums provide is meaning that they [the paintings] did not necessarily possess, then written interpretation may satisfy the need that both curators and visitors express, to control, tame, and diminish the effects of the instability of art. If, on the other hand, museums agree with Gumbrecht's interpretation of meaning and presence, as tension and oscillation, then interpretation might be seen as energising and provocative.

Stuart Hall says,

> Of course, there is no single or correct answer to the question, what does this image mean? ... since there is no law that can guarantee that things will have "one true meaning", or that things won't change over time, work in this area is bound to be interpretative, not simply a debate around who is "right" and who is "wrong" but between equally plausible, though sometimes competing and contested meanings and interpretations. The best way to evaluate contested readings is to look again at the concrete example and try to justify one's reading in relation to the actual practices and forms of signification used, and what meanings they seem to you to be producing.[36]

Often a simple conversation about artworks in the gallery will result in a more energised, lively discussion, a more personal interaction that opens up possibilities for a very different experience to that provided by text communicated as institutional opinion. As Ricœur says,

> the relation between message and speaker at one end of the communication chain and the relation between message and hearer at the other are together deeply transformed when the face-to-face relation is replaced by the more complex relation of reading to writing.[37]

The act of curating is an exercise in conceptual, contextual, and historical sorting, and each step in the process contributes to the shaping of its reception. The act of selecting a work for acquisition implies value and status, positioning it in a specific display connects it to a family or group, and establishes it within a broader political, economic, and social framework. These decisions frame the conditions around which the work will be understood. Text is one step in the journey but a particularly important one. Just as a curator selects artworks to tell a story, text has its own agenda. It is communicated and packaged as explanation, delivered to the visitor in more easily understandable language. Expanded labels and wall panels are sometimes criticised for their subjective tone but is hard to imagine how a discussion of an artwork could offer anything other than a subjective opinion, "Even when a narrative aspires to be neutral and objective, closer scrutiny reveals the presence of a voice or viewpoint with distinct characteristics".[38] Whether the interpreter chooses to write text that "serves a work by willingly providing the expected commentary or, conversely, dominates it by imposing his/her own view",[39] the new text will always intervene and will always be as subjective as the visual text to which it speaks, sometimes even competing with the subject of its interpretative analysis leaving those engaged in writing text *for* image in the ambiguous position of also writing *against* it, so that, "works [lose] their formal autonomy and became incommunicable except through commentary ... [competing] with art itself."

Inevitably, any interpretation provided by a museum will be influenced by individual curators' history, background, and education and interventions of this kind can never be neutral. Text can never exempt itself from its own contextualisation and from the requirement that it too, like the visual text upon which it seeks to elaborate, will be subjective and personal. Believing that text is objective assumes that interpreters are able "to stand outside ... [of their] beliefs in a neutral encounter".[40] It would be difficult, maybe even impossible, to imagine the kind of situation Mailloux describes here; one in which interpreters stand outside of their beliefs in a neutral encounter.

Just as text will always be subjective, interpretation can never be found in a single truth, "anyone who strives to reach the true interpretation of a work subscribes to the idea that it has a sole interpretation. Any other that claims to be true is written off as fantasy, falsehood, lie".[41] There is no truth in interpretation and no objectivity either,

> there can be no objective way of judging the relationship between a representation and what it purports to represent, since what is seen as reality in a given culture is definable only in terms of its specific modes of representation.[42]

40 *Interpretation and Text*

And works of art have their own context, their own baggage. They do not exist in a space that is unaffected by external social or cultural forces but are always,

> not only reflecting its context but mediating it, reflecting upon it; and the work is understood as not simply passive with regard to the cultural forces that have shaped it, but active – producing its own range of social effects, and acting upon its surrounding world.[43]

Museums and galleries are in a difficult position: if the text they provide is a structured analysis of the formal elements of a work, its colour, composition, and form, they may alienate those for whom feeling is of fundamental importance. If, however, they choose an interpretation that is informed by, "Kant's understanding of disinterestedness, requiring no concern for the real existence of the thing … only a pleasure arising from the object's universally apprehended form",[44] they may be criticised for taking an obscure and elitist approach. Meaning, it seems will always occupy a central role as it "presupposes a discrepancy between the clear meaning of the text and the demands of [later] readers … and seeks to resolve that discrepancy".[45] Preziosi might be right in suggesting that,

> an artwork [would] be mute or illegible without a certain kind of staging, but is an artwork ever "not framed", whether materially or virtually, "does it not swim or sit or hang suspended in an ocean of verbiage which may at times be palpably embodied in a visible gloss of words on a wall or pedestal or in your ear?"[46]

I want to continue with this discussion regarding the formal structure, the line, shape, colour, and form of a painting and ask whether this material expression of form can ever have its own agency and communicate its own meaning. Can a painting do what Mitchell suggests, "exhibit physical and virtual bodies; [that] speak to us, sometimes literally, sometimes figuratively: or [do they] look back at us silently across a gulf unabridged by language".[47] I am very drawn to the idea of a picture having needs and desires, but this poses even more questions about artistic intention. Hirsch writes about the relationship of meaning to interpretation from a literary perspective,

> I am not now, nor have I ever been a proponent of a moment of interpretation before intention is present … phonemes and

graphemes become signifiers only when they acquire meanings, and when they lose their meanings, they stop being signifiers.[48]

Hirsch suggests that the phonemes and graphemes of writing "become signifiers only when they acquire meaning". In a similar way, the marks, colours, and form of a painting might only become signifiers when they acquire meaning. How that meaning is formed and how it is communicated, whether it is embedded within the words of the museum curator, or in the presence and nature of the works' physical properties, is central to the debate.

The museum visitor loves interpretative text and complains bitterly if it is not available, (a questionnaire given to visitors to the Rothko exhibition in 2008, revealed that "over eighty per cent said that they were planning to read the wall texts".[49] They speak of it as transformative. One visitor told me that after reading that a certain painting was produced in 1946, she saw it differently with elements of war. Indeed, during many informal conversations with visitors I was struck with how strongly influenced they were by what they were reading, almost as if it offered them an alternative to the act of confronting an image, alone and unaided. Bryson says: "It cannot be taken for granted that the evidence which makes up 'context' is going to be any simpler than the visual or the verbal text on which such evidence is to operate".[50] Despite this, interpretation is thriving. Epistemological uncertainly seems to have given rise to ever more complex, even more lengthy, captions, wall texts, and room panels, reminding me of people speaking very loudly when they think that someone has not quite understood their point. Front of house management use the provision of text as proof of their commitment to accessibility and inclusivity, learning departments believe that text is the most effective way to 'speak' to visitors from every level of society, class, and education, press and media use text as a marketing tool and curators produce erudite catalogue essays, most often for other curators and to further their careers.

At the end of the Tate Britain 2010 conference, *Interpretation, Theory and the Encounter*, I asked Donald Preziosi to define the museum space. He replied that it is "a space where both what is staged and the staging itself are productive of knowledge: where there is little that is not potentially interpretative whether by design or appropriation".[51] Written interpretation is positioned within a space, which is itself a site of staging as well as a home for whatever is being staged: a space where every aspect of its being, the building, structure, and content is interpretative.

Changes in attitude to text has been the focus of this chapter. Museums are themselves a form of writing ... staging and framing too. Text is involved in every aspect of the building, the space, orientation, organisation, arrangement, display. It is a written manifesto of the museums' philosophy and contributes to its ideology.

Museums exist because that is where objects deemed worthy of being preserved for future generations are kept. Museums are run by curators and conservators – people who usually have degrees in art history. Not only are they the guardians of objects, but they wrap them in texts: interpretative texts, texts that attribute and identify, historical and critical interpretations, social histories.[52]

"Museum texts [are] a central component of a museum's communication agenda"[53] and in the act of providing that text, the gallery inevitably intervenes between the artwork and the viewer, and the nature of that intervention is constructed and communicated in the gallery's own terms, and becomes part of the gallery's authoritative power, its communicative strategy and as such, an institutional directive for how we should look and understand.

Notes

1 Edward Said, "Opponents, Audiences, Constituencies and Community" in *The Politics of Interpretation*, ed. W. J. T. Mitchell (Chicago: University of Chicago Press, 1983), 7.
2 The 1995 leaflet that accompanied *New Displays* states that this initiative will "enable more people to see works of art which would otherwise remain in storage".
3 Michael Grenfell and Cheryl Hardy, *Art Rules: Pierre Bourdieu and the Visual Arts* (New York: Berg, 2007), 81.
4 Nicholas Wroe, "The hanging judge", *The Guardian*, 22 April 2000, www.theguardian.com/culture/2000/apr/22/art.tatebritain
5 Elizabeth Fullerton, "Tate Director Chris Dercon: 'Everything can be changed'" *ARTnews*, 27 February 2013, www.artnews.com/art-news/news/tate-director-chris-derco-2166/
6 An essay by Rosalind Krauss originally published as "Le Musée sans murs du postmodernisme," *L'Oeuvre et son accrochage*, special issue of *Cahiers du Musée nationale d'art moderne*, 17–18 (1986): 152–158.
7 Louisa Buck, "The Work of Art as Time Traveller", *The Art Newspaper* 103 (2000): 42–44; see also Iwona Blazwick and Simon Wilson eds. *Tate Modern: The Handbook* (London: Tate Publishing, 2000), 30–35.
8 Donald Preziosi, *Rethinking Art History: Meditations on a Coy Science* (New Haven: Yale University Press, 1989), 83.

9   Tate annual report, 1998, https://assets.publishing.service.gov.uk/governm ent/uploads/system/uploads/attachment_data/file/235376/0912.pdf
10 Simon Wilson was the curator of Interpretation at Tate from 1991.
11 Louise Jury, "'I am the public's defender and my mission is to explain'; Louise Jury meets the gallery's curator of Interpretation", *The Independent*, 18 July 1999.
12 Terry Eagleton, *Literary Theory: An Introduction* (Oxford: Blackwell, 1983).
13 Beverly Serrell, *Exhibit Labels: An Interpretive Approach*, 2nd ed. (Lanham: Rowman & Littlefield, 2015), 7.
14 Sylvia Lahav, *Interpretation in the Art Museum: Authority and Access* (PhD diss, Institute of Education, University of London, 2011), 268.
15 Tate's unpublished guidelines for writing labels, 2008.
16 Lahav, *Interpretation in the Art Museum*.
17 Norman Bryson, "Art in Context" in *The Point of Theory: Practices of Cultural Analysis*, eds. Mieke Bal and Inge E. Boer (Amsterdam: Amsterdam University Press, 1994), 65.
18 Bryson, "Art in Context", 66.
19 Matisse quoted in Charles Harrison, Paul Wood, and Jason Gaiger, eds. *Art in Theory, 1815–1900: An Anthology of Changing Ideas* (Oxford: Blackwell, 1998), 72.
20 Mieke Bal, *A Mieke Bal Reader* (Chicago: University of Chicago Press, 2006), 214.
21 Frances Bacon interview with David Sylvester recorded by the BBC in October 1962 https://theoria.art-zoo.com/interview-with-david-sylvester-francis-bacon.
22 Hans Maes, "Intention, Interpretation, and Contemporary Visual Art" *The British Journal of Aesthetics* vol. 50, no. 2 (2010): 121.
23 Donald Prezioisi, "Palpable and mute as a globed fruit" *Tate Papers* 15 (2011) www.tate.org.uk/research/tate-papers/15/palpable-and-mue-as-a-glo bed-fruit
24 Andrea Giunta, "The Power of Interpretation (or How MoMA Explained Guernica to its Audience)", translated by Jane Brodie, Après le paysage: l'art, l'inscription et la représentation de la nature en Amérique latine aujourd'hui, *Artelogie* no. 10 (2017). https://doi.org/10.4000/artelogie.953
25 Keith Moxey, "Visual Studies and the Iconic Turn", *Journal of Visual Culture* vol. 7, no. 2 (2008): 132.
26 Giunta, "The Power of Interpretation".
27 Roland Barthes, "The Death of the Author" in *Image, Music, Text*, trans. Stephen Heath (London: Fontana, 1977), 146.
28 Roland Barthes, *A Lovers Discourse: Fragments*, trans. Richard Howard, (New York: Hill and Wang, 1974), 112.
29 Paul Ricœur, *Interpretation Theory: Discourse and the Surplus of Meaning* (Fort Worth: Texas Christian University Press, 1976), 4.
30 An idea taken from Abrams and quoted by Stanley Fish in *Is There a Text in This Class?: The Authority of Interpretive Communities* (Cambridge: Harvard University Press, 1980), 303.

44 *Interpretation and Text*

31 Bryson, "Art in Context", 66.
32 Christian Thiel, *Sense and Reference in Frege's Logic* (Blakeley: Reidel, 1968).
33 Hans Ulrich Gumbrecht, *Production of Presence: What Meaning Cannot Convey* (Stanford: Stanford University Press, 2004), 21.
34 In Walter Benjamin, *The Work of Art in the Age of Mechanical Reproduction*, trans. J. A. Underwood (London: Penguin, 2008). Benjamin refers to woven text and fresh text.
35 Gumbrecht, *Production of Presence*, 108.
36 Stuart Hall quoted in Gillian Rose, *Visual Methodologies: An Introduction to the Interpretation of Visual Materials*, 2nd ed. (London: SAGE, 2007), 14.
37 Paul Ricœur, *A Ricoeur Reader: Reflection and Imagination*, ed. Mario J. Valdés (New York, London: Harvester Wheatsheaf, 1991), 29.
38 Mieke Bal and Norman Bryson, *Looking In: The Art of Viewing* (London: Routledge, 2001), 12.
39 Hans Belting, *Art History after Modernism* (Chicago: University of Chicago Press, 2003), 17.
40 Mailloux in W. J. T. Mitchell, *Against Theory: Literary Studies and the New Pragmatism* (Chicago, University of Chicago Press, 1985), 67.
41 Giunta, "The Power of Interpretation".
42 Martin Kemp, "Relativity not Relativism: Some Thoughts on the Histories of Science and Art, Having Reread Panofsky" in *Meaning in the Visual Arts: Views from the Outside: A Centennial Commemoration of Erwin Panofsky*, ed. Irving Lavin, (Princeton: The Institute for Advanced Study, 1995), 234.
43 Bryson, "Art in Context", 66.
44 Jonathan Gilmore, "Censorship, Autonomy and Artistic Form" in *Art History, Aesthetics, Visual Studies*, eds. Michael Ann Holly and Keith Moxey (New Haven: Yale University Press, 2002), 109.
45 Susan Sontag, *Against Interpretation* (London: Vintage, 1994), 6.
46 Preziosi, "Palpable and mute as a globed fruit".
47 W. J. T. Mitchell, *What Do Pictures Want?: The Lives and Loves of Images* (Chicago: University of Chicago Press, 2005), 30.
48 Hirsch in Mitchell, *Against Theory*, 49.
49 Minnie Scott, "Behind the scenes: Interpretation", accessed 7 November 2022 www.tate.org.uk/about-us/working-at-tate/behind-scenes-interpretation
50 Bal and Bryson, *Looking In*, 67.
51 This was said to me in a private conversation with Donald Preziosi.
52 James Elkins, *Art History versus Aesthetics*, (New York: Routledge, 2006), 59–60.
53 Louise Ravelli, *Museum Texts: Communication Frameworks* (London; New York: Routledge, 2006), 3.

3 Space and Place

So far, in this short book I have considered the disciplines of curating and interpretation. I have examined conflicting modes of operational functionality in the governance and maintenance of the permanent collection and compared this to the expansion and status of exhibition making. I have suggested that the modern museum is keen to imagine alternative spaces for participation and interaction and a new curatorial role for visitors. I have also discussed text-based interpretation, examined the value and nature of this form of specialist writing and questioned what it is, who writes it, and whether it meets visitor expectations.

This chapter is about the museum space, about place and emplacement. Here, I am particularly interested in Foucault's heterotopias and how this concept might be used to re-imagine new spaces in the museum given the limitations and restrictions of what is essentially a finite environment. I will suggest that, like curating, museums must reconcile their aspirations to become a space "in which time never stops building up and topping its own summit" with time at "its most flowing, transitory and precarious".[1] Evoking notions of time as precarious and transitory might also be used to describe a festival or fairground displaying the marvellous, weird, exotic, and extraordinary. Establishing a dialogue between these two very different time-related concepts will require alternative methodologies and a re-visioning of purpose, possibly even a new building or renovation of a space that hovers between the two, connected but also disconnected, part of, but also apart from. I will suggest that a successful example of this heterotopic space where two concepts of time are allowed to coexist is Tate's Turbine Hall.

From the start, the Turbine Hall exuded a very special atmosphere with its grand expanse of concrete, massive height, and generous dimensions of width and breadth.[2] Inspired by the street and avenue,

DOI: 10.4324/9781003213130-4

it offered visitors a connection with the outside, a space for the city to flood in.[3] Originally designed as a point of visitor orientation, this covered but open area with its entrance via a sloping ramp gave visitors the freedom to experience the space exactly as they wished, with no demands on them to visit any other part of the building. I like to think of it as an example of the new "front room, the place in a household which attempts to give palpable expression to its host's social and political aspirations, somewhere to impress the neighbours and overawe the country cousins"[4] and its sheer scale and vastness meant that even with huge visitor numbers, the building comfortably absorbed them.[5]

Described by Martin Gayford as "startling and novel … an unprecedented space for the display of art",[6] it quickly became Tate Modern's most iconic feature. I often wondered whether it was the dramatic descendance of the ramp that led to its rapid ascendence as star of the Tate Modern show. In truth, nothing prepared those of us working there, for such an enthusiastic and positive public response. What it was that so captured the imagination of visitors is hard to put into words, but inclusiveness, generosity, and accessibility were often mentioned. For me, waiting in the Turbine Hall on 12 May 2000 as the doors opened for the very first time, there was a real sense of expectation, drama, and excitement on the faces of those first delighted visitors.

In contrast to what seemed to be overwhelming approval for the ramp like entrance, the actual gallery spaces were less enthusiastically received, "the galleries for showing art were often the least successful spaces in the building".[7] Many visitors experienced the sequences of near identical, characterless, white-enclosures like directional points on a map moving people from space to space and encouraging a visiting pattern that resembled a

> visual movement … a constant decentering … the continual pull of something else, another exhibit, another relationship, another formal order, inserted within this one in a gesture which is simultaneously one of interest and of distraction: the serendipitous discovery of the museum as flea-market.[8]

The layout of individual galleries was largely determined by the dominant east/west axis of the building with four themes acting as 'strapline' identifiers for each suite. Visitors were able to see a selection of work from the twentieth and twenty-first centuries in a relatively limited number of rooms, rather than attempting to see the entire collection, a decision that perfectly suited a free entrance museum that hoped to encourage visitors to make multiple visits rather than embark on an exhausting 'once in a lifetime' marathon. In addition, opting for a thematic rather than a chronological hang gave curators the freedom to select work using criteria that was not restricted to chronological time or art historical genre. Inevitably, this arrangement did not meet with everyone's approval and artists and students were particularly dismayed and irritated by the annoying hurdles they had to negotiate, in order to guess in which themed display a specific artist might be located. Jed Perl described the hang as "choreographed by curators who choose to offer us art in their own newly devised patterns of theme and contrast, splicing and dicing art works into a kind of visual MTV".[9] This rather scathing attack was ironically quite close to Tate's stated ambition to provide a "zone of the flaneur, the aimless stroller … those who dip in and out of a cultural maelstrom".[10] Rebranding the museum as a marketplace rather than an archive or library was a conscious decision, intended to offer a less formal approach to exhibitions and display. Cynics, however, viewed the thematic hang as an institutional ploy to divert attention away from any gaps in Tate's historic collecting policy.

Many visitors choose a single suite of rooms then negotiated the galleries like "a processional path that tie[d] spaces together, each room, a separate chapter, but all of them articulating the unfolding of the master plot".[11] In her essay "Postmodernism's Museum Without Walls", Rosalind Krauss used this description for traditional museums like the Uffizi, The Louvre, The Metropolitan Museum of Art, or National Gallery Washington. Tate Modern had no aspirations to replicate the classical grandeur or strict order of these iconic buildings but nevertheless, the suggestion to follow a processional path was in some ways, just as apt, maybe even more so, and reference to an unfolding of the master plot was a beguiling concept for a modern art museum. What the plot might be, who had masterminded it, and how it might reveal itself are questions that have shaped and will continue to shape the future of art history. At Tate, it was the attitude of the director, curators, architects, and policymakers that created a new art historical trajectory, a new processional path, and a new space for interaction and participation, all of which have become the form of this, and many other museums.

The thinking behind the design of the internal spaces in Tate Modern was both practical and ideological. The permanent collection was shown on levels three and five[12] and sandwiched between, on level four, were the fee-paying exhibitions. This arrangement was a deliberate act, intended to emphasise the importance and influence of the permanent collection on temporary exhibitions.[13] An impressively long escalator transported people from the turbine hall to the first level of galleries bypassing the auditorium and café. This escalator controlled the flow of visitors, taking them directly from the street into the heart of the collection. It was also a moving platform for viewing and spectatorship. It was no surprise that the top two levels, located in the light beam had the best views of London and became the home of the two most profitable wings of the Tate Modern enterprise, the restaurant and members' room. It was also no surprise that education and learning spaces, seminar rooms and study areas were situated in the basement, at the east end of the Turbine Hall.

It was hoped that the Turbine Hall would successfully generate "a perfect marriage of architectural ambition and institutional desire on the one hand, and architectural achievements and institutional triumphs on the other, allowing both the institution and the building to emerge as vastly successful".[14] Whether we wholeheartedly agree with this glowing assessment is a matter of opinion but a dual focus on both the institution and the building interests me and I want to use these two features to evaluate how far Tate Modern has travelled to establish itself as the home of an accumulative historical survey, an extension of the cabinet of curiosity, and a space for individual creativity and interaction.

The Turbine Hall is a repository of memories, indentations, experiences, and encounters. It is also a space for emplacement, an empty stage where anything can happen, and something must happen.[15] As such, it can function both as the epicentre of activity and a metaphorical blank canvas, a pregnant space waiting for something to occur, a receptacle for magic to take place, and where visitors, in their role as newly emancipated subjects of participation, are empowered by physical or symbolic acts of interaction that enable them to determine their own social and political reality.[16] It is a space that is mediated, appropriated, and active in the formation of an institutional identity and might well be described as heterotopic, a space within a space, a site of (inter)action, participation, and physicality, an extension of educational exchange, a tool of communication and phenomenal spirituality.

It is also heavily branded and sponsored, a shop window that symbolises "the final capitulation of installation art to the culture industry. Once a marginal practice that subverted the market by being difficult – if not impossible – to sell, it is now central to the Tate brand".[17] As a separate but connected alternative space, it resists formal categorisation. It was never thought of as a cabinet of curiosity or an environment that charts a theorised exhibition story, it had no ambition to offer visitors a classical route or embark on a methodical journey from one art historical moment to another. It is quite literally, something else, an empty stage, a space in waiting that is open and free, a space of "burnished neutrality"[18] that makes no attempt to "dictate to those who enter, how they should experience it",[19] but to offer instead somewhere for visitors to have the participation and involvement they expect and the curatorial role they crave.

Early in the Tate Modern story, this space in waiting was given a financial injection of £4.4 million in the form of a sponsorship deal with Unilever.[20] This collaboration gave Tate the freedom to commission cutting-edge, international, site-specific work and transform the turbine hall from a basic point of orientation, to the popular 'must see' destination that it soon became, a multi-purpose environment that was part fairground, part playground, part stage, part laboratory, and part exhibition. Sometimes attitude will never become form and Serota's insistence that there was no requirement or expectation for selected artworks to necessarily fill the enormous dimensions was a case in point, as most artists took the view that the majesty of this expansive area could only be matched with "an art of size ... to make a big splash in the global pond of spectacle culture today, you have to have a big rock to drop".[21]

There was no overall curator for the Unilever series: Jessica Morgan selected three of the artists; Juliet Bingham oversaw Ai Weiwei's Sunflower Seeds; Donna De Salva installed Anish Kapoor's Marsyas; and Susan May worked with Olafur Eliasson and his Weather Project. Of the eleven commissioned works, nine included interactive elements: Louise Bourgeois' *I Do, I Undo, I Redo*; Bruce Nauman's *Soundscapes*; Carsten Höller's *Test Site*; Olafur Elliason's The *Weather Project*; Ai Weiwei's *Sunflower Seeds*; and Tino Sehgal's *These Associations* all invited and indeed, expected, the public to be part of the work. In each, there was a different point of entry and possible level of engagement. Olafur Eliason's *Weather Project* encouraged visitors to experience the sublime and engage with the brilliant light and warmth of the sun and potential of drizzly rain by lying flat out on the floor; Bruce Nauman explored his fascination with language and the human voice in *Raw Materials*, an installation of 22 sound recordings wrapped around the vast space; Doris Salcedo's *Shibboleth* created a fissure which meandered across the Turbine Hall presenting a metaphor for the history of racism and inequalities that exist between rich and poor in northern and southern hemispheres; and Juan Munoz's *Double Bind* employed visual and psychological games to create a series of intriguing scenarios playing on perspective and illusion, visibility, and invisibility.

Although each work was unique, occupying the same location and branded with the name of a single sponsor, gave it a unifying factor and very often installations were referred to, as Tate's Unilever or Tate's Hyundai commission. But that was where the generalisation ended. Descriptions of the work chosen used a variety of art historical terms, installation art, interactive art, participatory art, political art, sound art, and art of the spectacle, but to borrow from Bruce Ferguson's analysis of Rebecca Horn's, *The Glance of Infinity*,

> Dependable explanations are circumvented by [the] work's material and conceptual complexities which resist the very foundations of any disciplinary knowledge. No art-historical parameters, no sculptural stylistics, no performative affiliations, no cinematic genre, no intellectual or political affiliation can hold this body of work easily and comfortably.[22]

I feel this also describes much of the work selected for the Turbine Hall space.

In contrast to the processional path of the permanent collection and the irregular, eclectic, and provocative design of the temporary exhibition, the Turbine Hall became a space of action, a laboratory where visitors could take an active role in the completion of work. Whether artists saw this as an act of transference, a relinquishment of power, and a democratisation of experience or whether they used the interactive element to cleverly exploit visitors and attract attention is questionable. Whatever the motivation, visitors enthusiastically accepted their new role, and the museum was complicit in the act. Visitors could become artists or curators or producers or all three, essentially they were central to the creative project. Everything was addressed to them, everything was intended for them, they participated in, and often even completed the work.

Turbine Hall installations imposed no conditions, they were not reliant on a single lens perspective or static encounter and the work displayed there was anything the artist wanted it to be: playful, cinematic, sculptural, immersive. Some of the work was interpreted as a symbolic indicator of a change of focus and attitude, an attempt to satisfy the disparate interests of different stakeholders, the architects, the institution, directors and politicians. It is the combination of building and institutional ambition, that I want to explore further, using three of the original Unilever commissions. All three reflect a change of institutional attitude that has subsequently shaped the content and framed the curatorial character of these installations as well as directly influencing future patterns of visitor participation and interaction.

Louise Bourgeois was the first Unilever commissioned artist. There were two elements to the work. *Maman*, a giant spider that was positioned on the bridge and three nine-meter towers called *I Do, I Undo, I Redo* located in the east section of the turbine hall. These three massive steel structures ascended high above the bridge, two of them wrapped (and potentially poised to trap) visitors inside a steel spiral staircase that led to a platform of engagement where intimate and revelatory meetings with strangers and friends could take place. In choosing to mount the stairs, visitors were symbolically fulfilling the contract that Bourgeois had set for them, to follow an architectural script and transform the museum experience into a religious ritual in both form and content.[23] Huge mirrors helped to broadcast these encounters and the whole spectacle became immersive both for those participating as well as those watching from the bridge. (Looking back, I am struck by the strong similarity that this work has with digital platforms like Facebook and Instagram where experiences are personal and intimate while at the same time, they are being shared with vast audiences). Mirrors have always played an important part in Bourgeois work,

> Mirror means the acceptance of the self. I have lived in a house without mirrors because I couldn't stand, I couldn't accept myself. The mirror was an enemy. Now, the mirror cannot be your enemy, the mirror has to be your friend, otherwise you are badly off.[24]

Bourgeois' apparent antagonistic relationship with the mirror becomes a metaphor for her relationship with her ('self'). Foucault also refers to mirrors but for him they function as a heterotopic trope where

> this place that I occupy at the moment when I look at myself in the glass [is] at once absolutely real, connected with all the space that surrounds it, and absolutely unreal, since in order to be perceived it has to pass through this virtual point which is over there.[25]

The experience of sitting on a high platform looking at a version of oneself as an image on the horizon and beyond, available for others in the same sphere to see, fits well with Foucault's ideas of real and unreal, embodiment, and out of body experience.

Like many of the Unilever artists, visitor participation has been fundamental to Bourgeois. Much of her work is a kind of mutual communication where the viewer ceases to be a mere addressee of the message[26] but is instead, embodied within choreographic acts of ascendance, phenomenological reflection, and overt spectacle. French philosopher and phenomenologist Maurice Merleau-Ponty writes, "spatial forms or distances are not so much relations between different points in objective space as they are relations between these points and a central perspective – our body".[27] Ponty's insistence that the self and the world are inextricably intertwined, is reflected in Bourgeois work and symbolic of her search to find a form of spirituality that relies on a human point of view and its mutability for a wider understanding of reality.

Test Site by Carsten Höller was chosen for the Unilever commission in 2006. Five tubular spiral slides started their journey at intersecting points in the Turbine Hall, each one providing a heightened level of fear and exhilaration. I only experienced the lower slide but even that was unnerving and sliding from level five, the highest, was described to me as physically and emotionally intense. For Höller "the outcome of the experience was entirely reliant on visitor participation".[28] He wanted visitors to act as agents, or quasi-agents and to see themselves not simply as an important part of the work, but as the work itself. His aim was to achieve a set of unique inner experiences and fully embrace the work's physical, spiritual, and intellectual dimensions. He described the reactions of those who experienced his slides as raw material, "I don't believe in the art object as such … I don't believe it works on its own".[29]

Some visitors described *Test Site* as a carnival ride, playful and enjoyable. For others it was a subversive endurance test that was both disconcerting and unnerving. Mark Windsor called it "a platform of interaction"[30] but using the word *platform* may be misleading. A platform is a static arena whereas this work involved intense physical movement, a constant shifting of perception and changing relationships. *Test Site* was more than just an intervention, it reached out with its unique tentacle-like structure, to connect, like veins to a placenta, the history and tradition of the permanent collection with the temporality and sense of spectacle provided by the Turbine Hall. It explored a form of modernity, that freely disrupts order and status, dislocates hierarchies and liberates a wilder more adventurous sense of self.

As I develop my proposition that the Turbine Hall has become a physical as well as an ideological space of access, inclusion, and participation, I want to pause for a moment and focus on the issue of access. It is an uncomfortable fact that many of the commissioned pieces required a type of physical interaction that rendered them unsuitable for those with mobility and/or anxiety issues including visitors in wheelchairs, the elderly, or fragile or those suffering from vertigo. Both Bourgeois and Höller attempted to address this by assuring those who were unable to fully participate that the work could be equally satisfying as a spectator. Visitors were told that watching the faces of those who were physically enjoying the slides for example was as fulfilling as actually experiencing it themselves. I see this as problematic as well as potentially misleading in that, it fundamentally shifts the ratio of "independence of its object to the interdependence of its recipients".[31] Finally, it is worth noting that one audience group that took full advantage of Test Site was younger visitors who were enthralled with the interactive element. There was a dramatic rise in school visits with many children massively enjoying the 'slides' as they were affectionately called, in a distinctly untheoretical way.[32]

Tino Sehgal's *These Associations* was the thirteenth and final work to be chosen for the Unilever series in 2012. There were no large sculptures in the Turbine Hall. There was nothing at all in the space except people. Some were visitors, others, part of a group of chosen participants (250 in all, 70 at any one time) hired to take part in the performance. *These Associations* addressed relationships between individuals, between groups, between dynamics and power, conformity and individualism, communality and intimacy, freedom, agency, passivity, and control. The script for each participant directed them to walk up and down at varying speeds with differing intensity, sometimes singing, sometimes engaging visitors in conversation. This might sound relatively casual but in fact it was carefully choreographed. Those taking part, Sehgal called them interpreters, were involved in group movement, (but not dance, he made that very clear). They were encouraged to work collectively, be mindful of group dynamics, occasionally creating triangles or other patterns of shape and form. They would occupy empty spaces, ensuring a distance between themselves and others and vary their movement and rhythm with different levels of acceleration and deceleration, sometimes moving extremely slowly, sometimes almost sprinting. Participants were also asked to initiate conversations centred on themes of arrival, belonging, admiration, and dissatisfaction but not the practicalities of making the overall piece or the nature of art.

Disassociating a piece from its institutional surroundings is an important aspect of Sehgal's work which might be seen as problematic given that, in using the Turbine Hall, Sehgal has agreed to work with Tate, an act which some might see as an acceptance of the power and influence of the museum's hierarchy and mechanisms. We know however, that this work, (indeed all his work) is entirely focused on the act of subverting the institution and destabilising the traditional view of art as inanimate object. It is a critique of the "ideological concerns against the hegemonic and ethically problematic Western celebration of the material object"[33] seeking a radical shift of power from institution to individual, allowing the visitor to take control and potentially challenge the holy sphere of memory and remembering. Critically, the role of the performer/participant dictates the *pace* as well as generates the *life* of the work, exploring themes of "the self as social being, the group, the individual, belonging and separation".[34] Sehgal maintains a fragile boundary between art and life and his work only fulfils its status as an artwork when it seduces the spectator into its performative iteration.

The ideological ban on the documentation that Sehgal imposes on his work means that there is no press release, no recordings, photographs, flyers at the door, signs on the wall or catalogues at any stage of the process, "he obsessively constructs a polished, impregnable closed system – protected by curators, gallerists, and press officers – in which the work evades documentation at all stages".[35] This places his work in a realm of present-[ness], something he calls a simultaneity of production and reproduction. I find myself strongly attracted to Sehgal's elevation of physical experience, especially since it leaves interpretation, as living memory, in a privileged position.

Whether work that has been displayed in the Turbine Hall is installation art, participative, interactive, performative, or community focused and whether the performers are the definition of the artwork, part of the artwork, "living sculptures"[36] or containers for the message of the artwork, are questions that achieve no consensus of opinion. Kabakov says, "the main actor in the total installation, the main centre toward which everything is addressed, for which everything is intended, is the viewer",[37] but it doesn't always feel as if this is the case. For me, the visitor always takes a secondary role while the artist is centre stage.

In the final part of this chapter, I want to link the concepts that Foucault uses to expand upon his notions of time and space and consider how these ideas might be relevant for the modern art museum.

Foucault suggests that we are living in an epoch of simultaneity, juxtaposition, the near and far, and the dispersed. He offers many examples of heterotopic spaces, each of which can only be understood in its own historical and cultural context, (the cemetery, the ship, the theatre, and the fairground). I think that we should add to this list, the inside/outside, opening and closing, playground/fairground space of difference that is Tate's Turbine Hall. There are, however, problems with this. Foucault died in 1984 and sites like the Turbine Hall were not as common then, as they are now but I am taking his reference to "counter-sites that are outside of all places and absolutely different from all the sites that they reflect and speak about"[38] as a modern interpretation.

In his essay *Des Espaces Autres*[39] he proposes that life is less like a development through time but more closely resembles a network that connects points and intersects with its own skein.[40] It is my belief that installations like Höller's *Test Site*, Eliasson's *Weather Project*, and

Doris Salcedo's *Shibboleth* are physical manifestations of Foucault's beliefs. They physically intersect with their own skein while at the same time, they offer a critique on the social, ecological, political, and art historical fabric of our time, they provide a metaphor for the dilemma of the modern museum and the problems of collecting and display. But above all, they attempt to reconfigure time and space. As Louise Bourgeois says, "Space is something that you have to define. Otherwise it is like anxiety, which is too vague".[41]

Foucault framed his theories around concepts of utopian and heterotopic space, "utopias are sites that have no real place. They act as a direct or inverted analogy with the real space of society, which they represent in either a perfected form, or turned upside down. Fundamentally they are unreal spaces".[42] In his view, heterotopias exist, they are real localisable spaces, designed into the very institution of society, spaces where culture is represented and neutralised but also reversed, contested, and inverted. I see the Turbine Hall as a hybrid of these two ideas; it is real, but 'other', a space of difference, central to Tate, which is an institution of power and cultural excellence, but also dislocated from it. It is a stage for constructed situations, for the juxtaposition of incompatible objects and discontinuous times, "a space of illusion that denounces all real space, all real emplacements ... as being even more illusory"[43] and visitors have themselves become living heterotopias, entities that are dislocated and disorientated from the space that is their cultural environment.

Many art historians have made a connection between Foucault's notion of a heterotopic space and the museum, but they rarely address how this new evocation might "shift the definition of the museum away from objects and collections ... towards difference".[44] I think this shift is long overdue. At this particular moment, at this particular time of epistemological uncertainty, we should take seriously the task of re-examining notions of truth and legacy and re-evaluate collections that were amassed at a very different time with very different values and beliefs.

I want to end this chapter, with a brief discussion of the changing role of museum architecture. In the eighteenth century, the museum's clear sense of purpose and power, its "moral, intellectual and cultural authority"[44] was expressed in its architecture, in grand classical buildings that celebrated past eras and cultural superiority. More recently, architects have begun to design buildings that serve different needs and reflect a different purpose. As historic establishments, museums must present themselves as encyclopaedic and forever accumulative, reflecting solidity, formality, logic, order, and gravitas but they must also provide space for the marvellous, exotic, and extraordinary in a playful, ludic, flexible, interactive environment. Making space for these disparate needs requires a new approach and revision of ideas, "methods of exhibition have changed, along with the nature of the encounter between spectator and object, often requiring altered spatial arrangements".[45] Architect of the V&A's new Sainsbury Gallery, Amanda Levete, describes her design for the new extension as "a perfect combination of old and new, a knitting together of a formal power station and a sculptural new building containing the Oval Gallery, which hosts site specific installations a la Tate Modern's Turbine Hall".[46]

The modern museum visitor is more educated, more knowing, and more confident. They want members rooms and entrances with style and personality, events and workshops, conferences, book launches, and guest lectures. They want more seating, better signage, exciting learning experiences, shopping, and refreshments and 'spill-out' areas where they can socialise and mingle. Serota says, "a building as complex as a museum has many different functions. At certain moments of the day, it is like a theatre, at others a cathedral. Some people would say that it is like a marketplace".[47] In *The Art Museum in Modern Times*, Saumarez Smith says that "he is deeply interested in how visitors use and experience art museums and how architects shape that experience".[48] This statement raises questions of action and intent. Do architects shape the museum according to visitor needs or has visitor behaviour forced a change of architectural design and practice? An article on the spatial constitution and functional organisation of museum architecture[49] refers to three main types of museum space: exhibition space, traffic space, and rest space but there are striking omissions in this list: information space, storage space, digital space, interactive and participatory space, and most importantly a space for critique, discourse, and discord must all be seen as central to the modern museum.

Successful public building projects of any type will always reflect the mission, aims and objectives of the commissioning institution, acknowledge the needs and expectations of the user/visitor and work within budgetary and financial guidelines. They must accept political pressure and be mindful of sustainability, social, and environmental issues. The art museum is not exempt from these requirements but in addition, it must also reflect changing attitudes to art history and cultural theory and break away from the rigidity and exclusivity that has become the hierarchical structure of the traditional canon of art. The museum must find its own unique way to become an encompassing signifier that is flexible and adaptable, "a cloth that can be gathered here, stretched there to accommodate a form whose mutations are linked to the changing character of capital, the state and public culture".[50]

Museums are perfectly positioned to become prime sites of revision. They are ideological structures that facilitate the transformation of passive consumer to active producer, from spectator to curator, from observer to artist. Above all, they are spaces of space: empty space, heterotopic space, breathing space, a space of history and legacy and a constant reminder of the privilege, class, and colonial attitudes that have shaped our permanent collections and remain shockingly inadequate as a view of global art history.

Notes

1 Michel Foucault and Jay Miskowiec, "Of Other Spaces" *Diacritics* vol. 16, no. 1 (1986): 22–27.
2 In my recollection the Turbine Hall was always part of the architectural plan but Jacques Herzog says, that the hall was "not in the brief, there was no requirement to have it, but it was given by the building". Rowan Moore, "Herzog and De Meuron, Tate Modern's architects on their radical new extension," *The Guardian*, 15 May 2016, www.theguardian.com/artanddes ign/2016/may/15/herzog-de-meuron-interview-tate-modern-switch-house-extension
3 Gerhard Mack, "Building for Art" *du* (May 2000): 54–55.
4 Rodney Mace, *Trafalgar Square: Emblem of Empire* (London: Lawrence and Wishart, 1976), 11.
5 Reference to the space is made by Ron Smith, quoted by Wouter Davidt in "The Vast and the Void: On Tate Modern's Turbine Hall and 'The Unilever Series'" *Footprints* vol. 1 (2007): 77.
6 Martin Gayford, "A New Space for a New Art" in *Tate Modern: The First Five Years* (London: Tate, 2005), 7–12.
7 Michael Craig Martin in *Tate Modern: The Handbook*, eds. Simon Wilson and Iwona Blazwick (London: Tate Gallery Publishing, 2000), 17.
8 Rosalind E. Krauss, "Postmodernism's Museum Without Walls" in *Thinking about Exhibitions*, eds. Reesa Greenberg, Bruce W. Ferguson, and Sandy Nairne (London: Routledge, 1996), 245.
9 Jed Perl, "Contemplation and Magic: On the Essence of the Museum" in *Oxford Slade Lecture Series* (Oxford: University of Oxford, 2002), 18.
10 *Tate Modern: The Handbook*, eds. Simon Wilson and Iwona Blazwick, 31.
11 Krauss, "Postmodernism's Museum Without Walls", 242.
12 These levels have since been changed to levels two and four.
13 In a telephone conversation I had with Frances Morris in May 2021, she placed great emphasis on the extremely important role the permanent collection had on temporary exhibitions.
14 Davidt, "The Vast and the Void", 77.

15 This is an idea that Peter Brook explores in *The Empty Space* (London: Nick Hern Books, 2019).
16 Sue Bell Yank, "The role of social art according to Bishop and Mouffe", 20 November 2009, https://suebellyank.com/2009/09/the-role-of-social-art-according-to-bishop-and-mouffe/
17 Claire Bishop, "But is it installation art?" *PR.I.C ora et labora* (blog), https://pric.wordpress.com/3-theory/claire-bishop-on-installations
18 Rosalind Krauss, "The Cultural Logic of the Late Capitalist Museum", *October* vol. 54 (1990): 3.
19 Rowan Moore, "Architecture in Motion" in *Tate Modern: The First Five Years*, ed. Martin Gayford (London: Tate, 2005), 30.
20 There were 13 commissioned projects during this period.
21 James Meyer, *ARTFORUM*, December 2000, www.artforum.com/print/200010/james-meyer-47753
22 Bruce Ferguson in *Rebecca Horn: the Glance of Infinity*, ed. Carl Haenlein (Zürich: Scalo, 1997), 33.
23 These ideas are explored in depth in Carol Duncan and Alan Wallach, "The Museum of Modern Art as Late Capitalist Ritual: An Iconographic Analysis" *Marxist Perspectives* vol. 1, no. 4 (1978): 29–51.
24 "Louise Bourgeois: The Complete Prints & Books: Cat. No. 544 Mirror for Red Room", Museum of Modern Art, accessed 7 November 2022 www.moma.org/s/lb/collection_lb/objbydate/objbydate_beginyr-1990_sov_page-827.html
25 Foucault and Miskowiec, "Of Other Spaces", 24.
26 Ideas expressed by Federico Sabatini in "Louise Bourgeois: An Existentialist Act of Self-Perception" *Nebula* vol. 4, no. 4 (2007): 7.
27 Maurice Merleau-Ponty and James M. Edie, *The Primacy of Perception, and Other Essays on Phenomenological Psychology, the Philosophy of Art, History and Politics*. Edited, with an introduction, by James M. Edie, xix, (Evanston: Northwestern University Press 1964), 5.
28 Mark Rappolt, "My Idea of Fun" *Art Review* no. 4 (2006): 50.
29 Alfred Gell, *Art and Agency: An Anthropological Theory* (Oxford: Clarendon, 1998), 28.
30 Mark Windsor, "Art of interaction: A theoretical examination of Carsten Höller's Test Site" *Tate Papers* 15 (2011) www.tate.org.uk/research/tate-papers/15/art-of-interaction-a-theoretical-examination-of-carsten-holler-test-site
31 Ibid.
32 Claire Bishop in *Artificial Hells: Participatory Art and the Politics of Spectatorship* (London: Verso, 2012), 25, speaks about Kester's aversion to dealing with the forms of specific work and the affective responses they elicit as equally crucial to the work's meaning.
33 Ibid.
34 Adrian Searle, "Tino Sehgal: *These Associations* – review," *The Guardian*, 23 July 2012, www.theguardian.com/artanddesign/2012/jul/23/tino-sehgal-these-associations-review

35 Claire Bishop, "No Pictures, Please: The Art of Tino Sehgal" *Artforum* vol. 43, no. 9 (2005): 215–217, 216.
36 Museum of Equality and Difference, "Tino Sehgal: Art and Memory Beyond Inanimate Materiality", 16 April 2019, https://moed.online/tino-sehgal-art-memory/
37 Claire Bishop. "But Is It Installation Art?" *Tate Etc.* no. 3 (2005), www.tate.org.uk/tate-etc/issue-3-spring-2005/it-installation-art
38 Foucault and Miskowiec, "Of Other Spaces", 24.
39 Foucault, Michel. "Of Other Spaces, Heterotopias". Translated from *Architecture, Mouvement, Continuité*, no. 5 (1984): 46–49.
40 Foucault and Miskowiec, "Of Other Spaces", 24.
41 At the opening of an exhibition of Louise Bourgeois work at the Fruitmarket Gallery in Edinburgh, Adrian Searle invited critics, artists and writers to provide a question for her. Adrian Searle, "Any answers?" *The Guardian*, 26 February 2004, www.theguardian.com/culture/2004/feb/26/1
42 Foucault and Miskowiec, "Of Other Spaces".
43 Beth Lord, "Foucault's Museum: Difference, Representation, and Genealogy" *Museum and Society* vol. 4, no. 1 (2006): 3.
44 Charles Saumarez Smith, *The Art Museum in Modern Times* (London: Thames and Hudson, 2021), 22.
45 Helen Searing, *Art Spaces: The Architecture of Four Tates* (London: Tate, 2004).
46 Emma O'Kelly, "Amanda Levente: The star architect behind the V&A's transformation," Knight Frank (blog), 18 September 2017, www.knightfrank.co.uk/blog/2017/09/18/amanda-levete-the-star-architect-behind-the-vas-transformation
47 Nicholas Serota, "Tate Frames Architecture" in Cynthia Davidson, Nicholas Serota, and Richard Burdett, "An Interview with Nicholas Serota and Richard Burdett" *ANY: Architecture New York* no. 13 (1996): 23–58. www.jstor.org/stable/41856807
48 Saumarez Smith, *The Art Museum in Modern Times*, 10.
49 Zao Li, Qiong Wei and Hao He, "A Brief Analysis of Spatial Constitution and Functional Organization of Museum Architecture: A Case Study on Museums in Hefei" *Frontiers of Architectural Research* vol. 2, no. 3 (2013): 354–361.
50 Jo-Anne Berelowitz quoted in Allan Wallach "The Museum of Modern Art: The Past's Future" *Journal of Design History* vol. 5, no. 3 (1992): 207.

4 The Will to Know

The deep connection that art history and museums have to colonisation is a relationship shaped by privilege, power, and selected knowledge, specifically Western knowledge. How museums were founded, how new work was acquired, how the canon of art history became the dominant system of value and classification, how ideals of nationalism were embedded in collections, how messages of imperialism were communicated, and how selected knowledge became accepted truth, are all attitudes that have become the form, and cultural identity of museums. In this chapter I will suggest that over and above issues of class, gender, ethnicity and privilege, restricted ownership, and selected access to knowledge are key issues in the decolonising debate.

Felix Ensslin talks about "the will to know".[1] Some people, an elite, had the right to exert the will to know and these were often the same people who occupied privileged positions in the world of collecting, display, curating, and writing about art. Ensslin says,

> one might even go as far as to say that the expansion of curating beyond the confines of the caretaking of museum collections is the pathway along which the will to knowledge has extended its expansion of the museum's original remit to include new exhibition space, new media space and new space for discourse.[2]

In Chapter 3, I proposed a Foucauldian interpretation of heterotopic space in relation to Tate Modern's Turbine Hall and suggested that the desire shown by visitors to experience space differently, to participate and engage with large-scale installations, continues to flourish and grow. I would therefore agree that the will to know (and its more inclusive form, the will to share), has been instrumental in the redesign and re-imagining of museum space. The will to know is also without doubt, fundamental to the disciplines of curating, collecting, and categorising. But the will to know is not without its own context. Whose 'will' are we talking about? What is available for us to 'know' now? What it is we wanted to know then and how might we be able to readdress things that historically we have chosen *not* to know. These are questions that are fundamental to museum history. Extending the parameters of knowledge should also include, "an active interrogation into the very democratizing elements – the free spaces, the explosion of new media, the predominance of post-colonial discourses that are both testimony and effect of this will to knowledge".[3]

Chapter 2 looked specifically at the type of writing positioned alongside works of art, institutional text written by professionals who *know*, for those who *want to know*. I emphasised, in this chapter how reliant the museum visitor has become on interpretation, how implicitly they believe its content, and how noticeable have been the effects of its growing dominance. There are also other forms of professional art writing and critical analysis, magazine and newspaper reviews, journal articles, media discussions, websites, and exhibition catalogues. Specialist journals like *Frieze*, *Art Review*, *ONCURATING*, *Aesthetica*, the *Art Newspaper*, *Art Forum*, *CURA*, and *Apollo* are all written by established writers, curators, and collectors who wish to communicate, "an approach within contemporary culture that, in wanting new potentials, embraces writing as a problematization of the object of art, its dissemination and forms of exhibition".[4] Art writing has become an established university discipline that offers students, "the practice and study of art writing involving creative, philosophical, critical and theoretical approaches to writing about, writing with, and writing as art"(Glasgow School of Art),[5] and "a grounding in the philosophical and historical bases of criticism, to improve both their writing and their seeing, and to provide sources that they can draw on for the rest of their lives"(The School of Visual Arts, New York).[6] We have seen a renaissance of interest in museum education with a proliferation of papers, conferences, and academic articles and organisations like Engage and Gem[7] have increased the promotion of opportunities for career development. Art writers who wish to work in the cultural sector are joining art institutions and contributing to specialist journals that address a series of regulative social, political, and artistic concepts. These writers aspire to become members of a professionalised discipline that will facilitate entry into a privileged space where they are encouraged to communicate "the supposedly authoritative narrative of those whose production was written elsewhere".[8]

It is precisely in the act of re-inscribing *a narrative whose production was written elsewhere* that Ennslin's reference to the democratising elements of the will to know sits rather uncomfortably with the clearly privileged professional spaces that constitute the parameters and practices of art writing where representation of those outside of the mainstream, the colonised, and marginalised is woefully inadequate.

As we saw in Chapter 2, museum text is multidimensional and multipurposeful: used in policy documents as justification that the museum has made a public commitment to inclusivity and accessibility; in advertising, to promote the growing number of activities and events on offer and in its more elevated form as verbal curating. Museums also use text as epistemological methodology for re-examining established art practice, reinterpreting and rewriting art history, and re-presenting colonial history in a more acceptable form so that it can be seen to address the current government's *retain and explain*[9] policy.

But like other forms of literary discourse, art writing is shaped by its own cultural, historical, and social context and has adapted and developed in response to these changes. As art criticism, it was a late achievement of the Enlightenment, the same era that considered colonisation to be rational, political, military, ideological, and humanitarian, a time of economic and violent actions of looting, profit, slavery, and exploitation of labour. Art criticism is now part of a very different historical moment, "based on cultural and economic capital, resulting in streams of power that are both formal (related to position and money) and symbolic (the order of appreciation, knowledge, visibility, and recognition)".[10] Modern forms of art writing have their roots in the values of cultural capital where "text, writers, and language are treated as commodities"[11] and the values of cultural capital are re-enforced in a way not dissimilar to the commodification of art where "the problem is no longer that art works will end up as commodities, but that they will start out as such",[12] (the brochure for the Global Art Forum of 2008, states simply that, that art is a business).[13]

In a chapter devoted to legacy and colonial attitudes, acknowledging the way in which art writing has been used to re-inscribe power is critical. It is precisely this act of re-inscribing institutional power that is deterring writers who are desperate, "to write (produce) without being inscribed (reproduced) in the dominant white structure and…without re-inscribing and reproducing what [is rebelled] against".[14] We have entered a moment in time in which "the authority of institutions is being called into question by people – once marginalized, now increasingly empowered – who say the narratives they represent no longer apply".[15]

Limited access to the world of art writing has inevitably shaped knowledge production. Our museums are full of professionals who are *not* writing on behalf of, or in the interests of, those who historically have had no voice at all. Who is allowed to write, what is written, and who gets published are questions that need to be urgently addressed,

> shouldn't the dialogue on decolonisation begin from the idea of the subject and a reflection on the framework of the discussion? And if so, why don't we start with decolonising art criticism...raising fundamental questions about how stories are told, what the platforms of dialogue are, how they function, and finally, who is allowed to speak.[16]

As we attempt to define the role of the museum, its permanence, and physical presence in buildings that were designed to house objects that were and still are (forever) visual expressions of a dominant culture, we must face the reality of the results of colonialism, that is, illegal and brutal methods of collecting. Many of our national museums were funded by wealthy collectors who used unethical means to acquire work for their collections. Sir Hans Sloane funded his collection which was eventually to become the foundation of the British Museum, with earnings from his wife's plantations in Jamaica where enslaved people were responsible for the production of sugar, coffee, cocoa, and other goods. Sloane profited from the reach of the British Empire sending collectors and travellers from all over the world to 'acquire' items for him. The Wallace Collection also has numerous examples of looted work like the Ashanti gold rings and ceremonial swords from Ghana that were taken from the Kumasi royal palace in the 1800s, and there are countless other museums that display with pride, work that has been acquired either on the back of slave trading or other violent and inappropriate actions.

What to do in response to this uncomfortable history and how to deal with demands for immediate repatriation and calls for everything illegally obtained to be sent back to the country from which it was stolen, looted, or inaccurately described as 'legally'[17] acquired, is more complicated. Even writing the phrase *sending back* feels wrong and of course it is, when applied to migrating people but cultural appropriation and attitudes towards the repatriation of cultural artefacts is very different. Some countries, France, Germany, Australia, and the United States have taken the decision to return small numbers of objects of outstanding importance[18] and in 2017, Emmanuel Macron stated, "I cannot accept that a large part of cultural heritage from several African countries is in France … in the next five years I want the conditions to be created for the temporary or permanent restitution of African patrimony to Africa".[19]

This firmly worded statement of intent by the French president is yet to be fulfilled, in fact until January 2020, only one work had been returned, and this was part of a five-year loan so more of a temporary restitution. Lengthy documents and reports have been commissioned, written, and enthusiastically received: the Hague Convention of 1954, Unesco 1970, Unidroit 1995, the French Sarr-Savoy Report & Restituting Colonial Artifacts,[20] and most recently the Reclaiming Restitution report[21] of 2022, but the number of objects under consideration for repatriation is still extremely small.

In the United Kingdom where statue law is written into museum policy, deaccession is allowed but only in very specific circumstances: if the work is a duplicate or so badly damaged that it is deemed to be useless, or it is a gift or bequest or purchased with specific legal conditions that insist that it remains in the collection. British Museum guidelines state, "The Trustees of the British Museum have a strong commitment to the integrity and global public value of the Collection, and do not normally deaccession objects from it".[22] In a radio interview in 1980, the then director Dr David Wilson was not embarrassed to claim that of the vast collection of the British Museum's over four million artefacts, only six might ever be considered for restitution and even then, only as a long-term loan. Other directors have referred to deaccession in similarly dismissive terms using pejorative language that reinforces colonial attitudes. In 2019, current British Museum director Hartwig Fischer described the taking of the Parthenon Marbles as a creative act[23] and V&A director, Tristram Hunt referred to the sacred objects pillaged in 1868 from Maqdala as contested heritage, adding that "to decolonize is to de-contextualise".[24] This is an attitude that seems to ignore the fact that context is constructed and like history, favours the powerful and dominant.[25]

But thankfully attitudes can, and will, change particularly when there is pressure from all sides of the debate. Professor Dan Hicks of Oxford University sees no reason why laws regarding deaccession cannot be changed, "there is nothing to stop the trustee body deciding to return items ... the public and professional debate about the Benin bronzes is over".[26] Directors, policy makers, and cultural leaders are also reviewing their position. In a recent statement Tristam Hunt proudly announced that he had negotiated a 'renewable cultural partnership' with Turkey, a loan signed off by the Arts Council to allow the return of a third-century marble head of Eros that was removed from a sarcophagus and Jonathan Williams, deputy director of the British Museum has spoken of a "Parthenon partnership" with Greece, a move towards the return of the contentious Elgin Marbles to Athens after more than 200 years.[27] In July and August 2022 Germany and Nigeria signed an agreement paving the way for a systematic return of the Benin Bronzes; the Horniman Museum in South London made a commitment to transfer ownership of 72 objects including 12 Benin bronzes to Nigeria and the Universities of Oxford and Cambridge pledged their intention, "to return hundreds of Benin Bronzes, opening the possibility of the largest repatriation of looted artifacts from the United Kingdom to date".[28]

Occasionally when a museum wishes to make use of the very limited powers of deaccession available to them, they use the phrase 'rightful ownership'. This happened in 2022 and involved the archive of a thousand documents and sketches of the studio of Francis Bacon originally owned by his friend Barry Joule but donated to the Tate in 2004. Tate has now decided to return these archival documents but its reasons for restitution are more to do with contested provenance than generosity, claiming that the Joule donation has been "researched by art historians, and this research has raised credible doubts about the nature and quality of the material".[29]

As a rule, Tate does not practice deaccession, "Tate has not deaccessioned any work that have entered its collection other than one duplicate print by Roy Lichtenstein"[30] but in the United States, and some countries in Europe, deaccessioning happens more frequently. In 1989 the Museum of Modern Art bought a major work, a portrait of the Postman Joseph Roulin by Van Gogh, but to do so it sold seven major works by de Chirico, Mondrian, Picasso, Monet, Kandinsky, and Renoir. And the Baltimore Museum defending their decision to sell some work in their 65 collection, claimed that they were "parting with the past to move forward into the future".[31] It is precisely acts like these, selling work to raise money to buy something deemed more desirable, that concerns those who are against deaccession. They worry that rogue trustees might try to dispose of a museum's valuable artworks for self-interest or sell them to compensate for poor financial management and this raises the issue of where ultimate responsibility for any decisions taken, might lie. Hunt believes that it should be museum trustees who take final decisions, rather than directors or senior management but I doubt whether this would radically alter the outcome.

As well as museum directors, cultural bodies like Arts Council England, the Museums Association,[32] and Gem[33] have been keen to emphasise their commitment to "unreservedly support initiatives to decolonise museums and their collections".[34] In 2020, ACE advertised a job, stating that,

> the overarching aim of this work is to create a comprehensive and practical resource for museums to support them in dealing

confidently and proactively with all aspects of restitution ... and guidelines to inform ethical and legal considerations and include case studies for how museums and galleries might navigate restitution claims and the return of art and artefacts.[35]

It has taken two years for this long-awaited guidance[36] to be published, prompting the *Museums Journal* to comment that,

> publication of the document was held back on several occasions due to its increased political sensitivity. A source told us it was likely that the resignation of Boris Johnson had provided a "window of opportunity" for the guidance to be published before a new prime minister and cabinet are in place.[36]

The debate has become even more complex as key terms are used without clear meaning. Repatriation is the process by which cultural objects are returned to a nation or state at the request of a government; restitution is the mechanism by which cultural objects are returned to an individual or a community; and reparation is a move (financial, ethical, material) to repair former injustices. As well as important semantic differences, there is an ongoing discussion about cultural nationalism and cultural internationalism. James Cuno suggests that it is highly reductive to condemn a collection solely because of its imperial connections. He refers to Edward Said's statement that

> partly because of empire, all cultures are involved in one another, none is single and pure, all are hybrid, heterogenous, extraordinarily differentiated and un-monolithic. Without encyclopaedic museums, one risks a hardening of views about one's own particular culture as being pure, essential, and organic, something into which one is born. The collective political risk of not having encyclopaedic museums is that culture becomes fixed national culture.[37]

Cuno is making the point that it is narrow and restrictive to see works of art as expressions of a specific nationality rather than as part of a wider global artistic expression, that we should think of cultural artefacts as shared culture that transcends borders.

In her keynote speech for Sharjah Art Foundation in March 2021, Francoise Verges refers to the issue of normality, by which she means the norms of the master, "we will not return to normal because normal was the problem ... the master's tools will never dismantle the masters house".[38] In this poetically worded statement Verges is suggesting that existing structures and systems of power will never disrupt the foundations and hierarchy of their own institutions. If the debate around the decolonisation of museums is only taking place *in* museums, themselves institutions of power and privilege, it seems very unlikely that any real change will take place. It also reminds me of Tuck and Yang's reference to settler and non-settler people.[39] If we imagine museum professionals as settlers, which they are, in terms of power, status, and wealth, then we must also accept that they are "effectively coterminous with that which is to be problematized, namely, settler colonial futurity".[40] They wish to reassert the hierarchy of domination, exposition, and object thinking that substantiates ownership and privilege.[41]

I have highlighted knowledge, privilege, and the will to know as theoretical positions that I believe are central to the decolonial debate as well as actively contributing to the history of museums and how they were established, how acquisitions were made, how art history was conceived, and how knowledge has been owned, managed, and adapted to suit an educational, cultural, preselected elite. In the early formation of the museum, great emphasis was placed on progress and nationhood and focused, more or less exclusively, on the Western canon. These allegiances were never hidden and there was no attempt to present things differently.

The structure of the museum has been enabled by colonialism, but the language of colonialism, its history, actions, and thinking cannot be seen as theory sealed in a hermetic box to be opened, examined, and understood as finite, a closed entity. The discourse of colonialism is an ongoing dialogue that interrogates not only the history but also the influence of colonial thinking. It is inextricably embedded in anti or post-colonial thinking, "the prefix in post coloniality is not meant to signal the end of the previous period but to stand for the sign of an emancipatory project, that is, it announces a goal yet to be realized".[42] It occupies "a virtual space ... of possibility and emergence ... it opens towards a future that will not repeat existing forms of sociality and oppressive power relations".[43] Post-colonial theory examines the effects of colonial rule on class, order, and ethnicity and addresses the way in which the society and culture of non-European peoples has been viewed from the perspective of Western cultural knowledge, creating separate identities for the coloniser and the colonised. The effects of this system of oppression are active and present in the racial/ethnic classification of people that was constructed to maintain the power structure of the coloniser.

Decolonial activism is attempting to reverse these inequalities, unravel political privilege, and establish equality in areas that have been historically marked by injustice but "the traditions of thought associated with postcolonialism and decoloniality are long-standing and diverse".[44] It is precisely the diverse nature of decolonial thinking that has stretched its meaning almost to breaking point and academics, Tuck and Yang, are worried about what they perceive to be an all too easy adoption of the phrase by a range of social and educational structures, advocacy, and scholarship and increasing numbers of calls to decolonise schools, decolonise student thinking, decolonise reading lists, and decolonise teaching methods. This, they think, is turning decolonisation into a metaphor, "a form of enclosure, dangerous in how it domesticates colonization. It is also a foreclosure, limiting in how it recapitulates dominant theories of social change".[45] I would agree with them. The word, decolonisation as a description for all forms of inequality and injustice in teaching, education and learning, moves it far away from its original meaning, *the repatriation of Indigenous land and life*. But I can see why this is an attractive route to take. There are many areas of education and learning that need revision: a stagnant curriculum, outmoded teaching practice, a reversal of dominant methodologies, and reassessment of museum collections, all areas where "the invizibilised dynamics of settler colonialism marks the organization, governance, curricula and assessment of compulsory learning".[45] In all of these areas, change is certainly necessary but is decolonising the most appropriate description? The very act of naming, using a form of political cartography that subordinates differences and radically destroys identities may not be the best way forward. We might instead, think of new mechanisms and new power arrangements that allow for "the recognition and undoing of the hierarchical structures of race, gender, heteropatriarchy and class that continues to control life, knowledge, spirituality and thought structures that are clearly intertwined with and constitutive of global capitalism and Western modernity".[46]

Until now, the decolonising debate has been most active in museums that house objects of spiritual, religious, and historical significance. This book is focused on a different type of space, the modern art museum and here I would suggest that the word intersectionality might better suit a discussion around change and reform. Intersectionality is defined as "an analytical tool that can only exist as activism, as praxis, as the process by which a theory, lessons, or skills are enacted, embodied, reified or realized".[47] The keywords here are activism and praxis. Using intersectionality as a lens, would facilitate an interrogation of the 'for' over the 'against' of decoloniality, "it is in the for, in the postures, processes and practices that disrupt, transgress, intervene and in-surge in, that mobilize, propose, provoke, activate, and construct an otherwise, that decoloniality is signified and given substance, meaning and form".[48] The museum is an ideological machine that must engage with its past and respond to its future. It must re-examine historic issues of knowledge, privilege, and power and embed new structures of equality of opportunity, ethnicity, and class.

When Françoise Vergès asks, "who is cleaning in the museum, who are the guards, what is the process of decision making and who set up the collection"?[49] she is highlighting the very considerable inequalities that still exist in the museum's hierarchical structure. The realisation that until relatively recently our art institutions were full of white Western dead male artists came as a shock to many who believed that art history was a truthful account and the artistic canon, a true mark of excellence. We now understand that our collections are visual expressions of past colonial attitudes, false records of the history of art, "incomplete, under-representative, in denial of voices and perspectives that have not been seen as mainstream, geographically, the 'conventional "centring" of art history in Europe and America and traditional "Western" methodologies' has become increasingly unsatisfactory".[50]

Tate is a good example of an institution that is owning its past, addressing inequality, and actively collecting work that represents a better male/female balance,

> women have been discriminated against for centuries, and major institutions have typically failed to support the careers of women artists working on the margins. The number of women artists in the collection has expanded exponentially, and half the rooms in the Natalie Bell Building are currently devoted to a sole female artist.[51]

As well as addressing gender imbalance, Tate is only too aware that its collection is a product of colonial attitudes,

> the founding of our gallery and the building of our collection are inextricably connected to Britain's colonial past, and we know there are uncomfortable and inappropriate images, ideas and histories in the past 500 years of art which need to be acknowledged and explored. We also recognise the intersections of race, gender, sexuality and class in the experience of inequality.[52]

Tate is also readdressing the equality and diversity of museum staff and has established a Race Equality Taskforce committed to an acceleration of progress towards becoming an anti-racist organisation and affecting structural as well as programming and content changes.

On one level, this shows real progress, but inequality of class and privilege is still very prevalent at managerial level. A quick glance at recent directorial and management appointments in major London museums from the 1980s to the early 2000s, reveals that a large proportion were males from Oxbridge, many from the world of politics, banking, finance, or media (most often the BBC). In museum governance, less than ten per cent of trustees on museum boards were of diverse ethnicity and seven out of ten were male. Most of the larger institutions have recently reviewed their boards and the ratio of males to females is now relatively healthy, Tate (five out of eleven), the British Museum (eight out of twenty) and the V&A (seven out of sixteen). However, there are other examples of possible misuse of power. Becoming a museum trustee is not a political role, even though appointments are undertaken by the Prime Minister but there is growing evidence of attempts by government to use the trustee role to bolster a particular political view. Two trustees, one from the Science Museum Group and one from Royal Museums Greenwich recently stood down in protest at governments' insistence that trustees individually and explicitly express their support for the retain and explain policy, which favours keeping and contextualising controversial monuments and statues. One of the trustees who chose to give up her role made clear that in her view, "any requirement which seeks to constrain the independent curatorial and interpretive work of national museums violates the long-established principle of arm's length bodies. Today it is contested heritage. Tomorrow it may be another issue" and Ahdaf Soueif resigned from her role as trustee on the board of the British Museum blaming, a cumulative sense of the museum's 'immovability' on questions such as its sponsorship by BP and the legacies of colonialism.[53]

Away from the museum, international art events like the Venice Biennale are addressing inequality and the wider parameters of the decolonising debate. Curator of the 56th Biennale, the late Okwui Enwenzor used the theme, *All the World's Futures* to frame what he called a "critique of the nationalism inherent to the Venice Biennale, and the role of nationalism in art history" but the Biennale is both specifically nationalistic and culturally international. The construction of national pavilions will always, in very concrete terms, represent a time when imperialism meant power, money, and dominance. Along with museums, curators of the Biennale are challenging colonial ideas and inequality of gender, race, ethnicity, and class (as far as it is possible). In the 2022 Biennale the New York-based Italian curator, Cecilia Alemani, selected more women (90%) than ever before to explore the world from a perspective other than that of the white male. But Yuki Kihara, representing Aotearoa New Zealand in her exhibition Paradise Camp has voiced reservations about using her as an ambassador and campaigner for women, for gender equality, for Trans rights, for "talking back to the canon"[54] and for challenging the image of the artist as a lone genius.

Whose culture, whose power, and whose reputation are not just context, they are central to the decolonising debate. The phrase, to *decolonise is to decontextualise* implies that context will somehow replace responsibility and alleviate blame for colonial action using the excuse of settler innocence. We must replace a negative denial and superficial abolishment of history (that can never be fully achieved), with a reactivation, re-mobilisation, (re)surgence of possibilities that are meaningful and possible, and this change must come from the bottom as well as the top of the power structure and include all aspects of museum management. We need to take an accumulative not a reductive approach to history and knowledge and weave into our present, aspects of our past that may be uncomfortable and will certainly impact on current attitudes. As Frantz Fanon comments, "colonisation comprises not only the intersection of historical and objective conditions but also man's attitude toward these conditions".[55]

The modern art museum must accept colonialism as a historical violence but also a modern attitude. We need to acknowledge that privilege, access to knowledge, and an incentivisation towards gaining knowledge, in other words the will to know, continues to frame the decolonising debate. Art and collections of art are not exempt from changes of attitude. We must own the injustices that have resulted in collections that say more about wealth, power, and privilege than about equality, access, and liberty and adjust our attitudinal position. We must think hard about where we have been and where we might want to go.

Legacy has never been neutral, never been equal, and never been representative. Our colonial past will forever influence our present and inform our future and legacy should never be seen as legitimacy in the history of the museum.

Notes

1 Felix Ensslin, "The Subject of Curating – Notes on the Path towards a Cultural Clinic of the Present", *OnCurating* no. 26 (2015): 21.
2 Ibid., 22.
3 Ibid., 20.
4 Maria Fusco, "11 Statements around Art Writing," *Frieze*, 10 October 2011, www.frieze.com/article/11-statements-around-art-writing

72 *The Will to Know*

5 "Art Writing", Glasgow School of Art, accessed 9 November 2022, www.gsa.ac.uk/study/graduate-degrees/art-writing/
6 "Announcement: Art Criticism & Writing, School of Visual Arts", *Art & Education*, 17 January 2012, www.artandeducation.net/announcements/109664/art-criticism-amp-writing-mfa-school-of-visual-arts
7 Engage, the lead advocacy and training network for gallery education was established in 1989, Gem was founded in 1948.
8 Spivak quoted in Gurminder K. Bhambra, "Postcolonial and Decolonial Dialogues" *Postcolonial Studies* vol. 17, no. 2 (2014): 117.
9 Boris Johnson's government adopted a 'retain and explain' policy on contested heritage that included writing to museums, galleries, and arm's length bodies advising that they do not remove contested heritage from their collections.
10 Zofia Cielatkowska, "Decolonising Art Criticism", *Kunstkritikk*, 10 January 2020.
11 Ibid.
12 Quoted in Robert McDougall, "Global art, post-colonialism and the end of art history (Robert McDougall), Part 1", *Esthesis*, 2 May 2020, https://esthesis.org/global-art-post-colonialism-and-the-end-of-art-history-thoughts-on-hans-belting-robert-mcdougall/
13 Program brochure to The Global Art Forum, 2008, 2
14 Walter Mignolo and Catherine E. Walsh, *On Decoloniality: Concepts, Analytics, and Praxis* (Durham: Duke University Press, 2018), 20, 21.
15 Andrew Goldstein, "Museums are contested sites. The Art Institute of Chicago's James Rondeau on why he finds the current moment so electrifying", Artnet News, 23 July 2019, https://news.artnet.com/the-big-interview/james-rondeau-art-institute-of-chicago-interview-part-1-1607410
16 Cielatkowska, "Decolonising Art Criticism".
17 The radio series Meridian (broadcast in June 1981) explores these issues in relation to treasures that were acquired legally and illegally.
18 United States has agreed to return 17,000 looted treasures to Iraq, Berlin 440 artefacts to Nigeria. *The Guardian*, 3 August 2021, "US to return 17,000 looted ancient artefacts to Iraq".
19 Tristram Hunt, "Should museums return their colonial artefacts?", *The Observer*, 29 June 2019, www.theguardian.com/culture/2019/jun/29/should-museums-return-their-colonial-artefacts.
20 Felwine Sarr and Bénédicte Savoy, *Rapport sur le restitution du patrimonie culturelle africain – Vers une nouvelle éthique relationelle* (2018), www.vie-publique.fr/rapport/38563-la-restitution-du-patrimoine-culturel-africain
21 The Reclaiming Restitution report states, "The restitution of African heritage – artefacts and human remains – is one of the vital social justice issues of our times. It is about recognising centuries of devastation of the African continent, and taking a step towards social, historical and cultural repair for Africans themselves". https://openrestitution.africa/reclaiming-restitution-report/

22 British Museum, British Museum policy: De-accession of objects from the collection (2018) www.britishmuseum.org/sites/default/files/2019-10/De-accession_Policy_Nov2018.pdf
23 This statement was made in an interview published in Ta Nea in January 2019. Mark Brown, "British Museum chief: Taking the Parthenon marbles was 'creative'", *The Guardian*, 28 January 2019, www.theguardian.com/artanddesign/2019/jan/28/british-museum-chief-taking-the-parthenon-marbles-was-creative
24 Hunt, "Should museums return their colonial artefacts?".
25 In 2018, the percentage of BME Chief Executives increased from 8% to 9%, Artistic Directors from 10% to 12% with the percentage of Chairs staying static at 10% in the last two years. *Call for more action on diversity and inclusion in the arts*, 19 February 2020, www.workingmums.co.uk/call-for-more-action-on-diversity-and-inclusion-in-the-arts/
26 Robbie Griffiths, "Londoner's Diary: Return of the Benin Bronzes turns heat up on British Museum", *Evening Standard*, 8 August 2022, www.standard.co.uk/news/londoners-diary/londoners-diary-british-museum-benin-gordon-brown-james-bond-jodie-comer-b1017223.html
27 Naomi Clarke, "British Museum executive calls for 'Parthenon partnership' over Elgin Marbles", *Evening Standard*, 31 July 2022, www.standard.co.uk/news/london/elgin-marbles-british-museum-parthenon-partnership-london-b1015777.html
28 Tessa Solomon, "Oxford and Cambridge will oversee likely largest UK repatriation of looted objects to Nigeria", *ArtNews*, 1 August 2022, www.artnews.com/art-news/news/oxford-and-cambridge-will-oversee-likely-largest-uk-repatriation-of-looted-objects-to-nigeria-1234635569/
29 Ibid.
30 Tate, *Tate Acquisition and Disposal Policy. Approved by the Board of Trustees on 18 November 2020* (2020) www.tate.org.uk/documents/1685/acquisition_and_disposal_policy_2020.pdf
31 Angelica Villa, "The most controversial U.S. museum deaccessions: Why do institutions sell art?", *ARTnews*, 26 October 2020, www.artnews.com/feature/most-controversial-museum-deaccessioning-plans-1234575019/
32 Museums Association, "Our response to the DCMS contested heritage meeting on 23 February", 24 February 2021, www.museumsassociation.org/campaigns/ethics/our-response-to-the-dcms-contested-heritage-meeting
33 Sonia Sharma, "Decolonising learning in museums", 30 September 2021, https://gem.org.uk/decolonising-learning
34 Museums Association, "Our statement on decolonisation", accessed 9 November 2022, www.museumsassociation.org/campaigns/decolonising-museums/our-statement-on-decolonisation.
35 Kate Fitz Gibbon, "Arts Council England: Guidelines for museum repatriation", *Cultural Property News*, 8 April 2020, https://culturalpropertynews.org/arts-council-england-guidelines-for-museum-repatriation-policy

36 Geraldine Kendall Adams, "Arts Council publishes long awaited restitution guidelines", Museums Association, 5 August 2022, www.museumsassociation.org/museums-journal/news/2022/08/arts-council-publishes-long-awaited-restitution-guidelines
37 Hunt, "Should museums return their colonial artefacts?".
38 Francoise Verges, "Dismantling the Master's House" (Keynote speech at the Sharjah Art Foundation March Meeting 2021), www.youtube.com/watch?v=2izb4OcnwzA
39 Eve Tuck and K. Wayne Yang, "Decolonization is not a metaphor", *Decolonization: Indigeneity, Education & Society* vol. 1, no. 1 (2012): 1–40.
40 Matthew P. Fitzpatrick, "Colonialism, Postcolonialism, and Decolonization", *Central European History* vol. 51, no. 1 (2014): 83–89.
41 Cielatkowska, "Decolonising Art Criticism".
42 Venn Couze, *The Postcolonial Challenge: Towards Alternative Worlds* (London: SAGE, 2006), 190.
43 Ibid., 190.
44 Bhambra, "Postcolonial and Decolonial Dialogues", 115.
45 Tuck and Yang, "Decolonization is not a metaphor", 3.
46 Mignolo and Walsh, *On Decoloniality: Concepts, Analytics, and Praxis*, 17.
47 Richard Haden, "Intersectionality in South Florida, June 16 – August 14, 2016", Museum of Contemporary Art North Miami, accessed 9 November 2022, https://mocanomi.org/2016/06/intersectionality
48 Mignolo and Walsh, *On Decoloniality: Concepts, Analytics, and Praxis*, 17.
49 Françoise Vergès, "Decolonizing the Museum?" *Frank Davis Memorial Lecture Series* (Courtauld Institute of Art), 6 October 2021, https://youtu.be/STi30reki38
50 Dr Mary Kelly and Dr Ceren Özpunar, "How can art history be decolonised?", *The British Academy* (blog), 10 June 2021, www.thebritishacademy.ac.uk/blog/how-can-art-history-be-decolonised/
51 "What does it mean to be a woman in art?", Tate, accessed 9 November 2022, www.tate.org.uk/art/women-in-art
52 "Our commitment to race equality", Tate, accessed 9 November 2022, www.tate.org.uk/about-us/our-commitment-race-equality
53 Charlotte Higgins, "How did Osborne, king of cuts, become the British Museum's fundraiser-in-chief?", *The Guardian,* 29 June 2021, www.theguardian.com/commentisfree/2021/jun/29/george-osborne-british-museum-arts
54 Jinghua Qian, "Fa'afafine Yuki Kihara celebrates Samoa's third gender: 'Galleries think they can tick the box with me'", *The Guardian*, 28 April 2022, www.theguardian.com/artanddesign/2022/apr/29/faafafine-yuki-kihara-celebrates-samoas-third-gender-galleries-think-they-can-tick-the-box-with-me
55 Frantz Fanon, *Black Skin White Masks* (London: Pluto, 1986), 65.

Looking Back ... Final Thoughts

There are no neat conclusions for a book such as this, only final thoughts.

I was lucky enough to work in Tate and other London galleries at a time when the United Kingdom was experiencing renewed interest and increased enthusiasm for all things creative and there were signs of growing confidence and optimism within the arts and culture sector. This was a moment that celebrated the beginning of a new century with substantial financial opportunities made possible by an injection of millennium funding that gave museums (and other cultural institutions) the opportunity to complete grand capital building projects and push forward their ambitious plans for exhibitions and displays and innovative interpretation and learning programmes.

It was also during these final two decades of the twentieth century, that museums began to re-evaluate their mission, their strategy, their management structure, and their working practice, partly to accommodate a demonstrable growth of interest and partly to offer proof to government that they were attracting a cross section of visitors of diverse ethnicity, education, and economic status, a stated prerequisite if they were to retain their free entrance status. It became a requirement that they contribute financially to their own upkeep, and this in turn gave rise to a new push towards entrepreneurial activity and more focus on income generation. The transformation from relatively passive institutions with scant information about visitor type, visitor interests, and visitor needs, to proactive, market-led organisations with detailed knowledge of their client base was liberating. There was a flurry of exciting exhibitions and events, innovative courses, lectures, workshops, more cafés, more shops, and more merchandising opportunities, all of which helped re-energise the form and function of the modern museum.

Being part of Tate, an establishment that was undergoing these radical changes, was an experience that I will always value and it is this, that has motivated me to write about how I saw things from within,

DOI: 10.4324/9781003213130-6

how the museum adapted to government requirements and differences in visitor behaviour and demands, how it managed to upgrade its offer and change its identity, how the status and character of exhibitions and displays presented new challenges and increased expectations, how doubts about the future of an encyclopaedic collection were regularly discussed, how divisions of institutional opinion about the growth and nature of interpretative text came into focus, how we developed impressive new museum spaces that gave visitors the opportunity to participate, interact and even co-curate art work, and how policy on equality, access, and diversity was updated and revised.

During this period, museums changed their attitude to visitors. The days of opening the doors at ten and closing them at six with little or no knowledge of who was visiting, why they were visiting and importantly who was *not* visiting, became a thing of the past. Museums realised that they needed data to support their claims that they were truly accessible and inclusive. They spent large sums of money on advertising, visitor surveys, audience profiling, evaluation, and visitor behavioural research so that they could learn more about what visitors wanted to see, when they wanted to visit, and how they wanted to use their time in the museum. They quickly understood that visitors expected different activities that suited their modern lifestyle and fitted the parameters of their leisure time. Above all, they wanted to be active rather than passive consumers, creative and artistic co- producers and knowledgeable and informed co-curators. They wanted real agency and the ability to influence decisions about how work was valued, how it was displayed, and how it was interpreted. They also wanted to take full advantage of as many of the opportunities to participate and interact that were offered to them.

Museums began to ask questions of museum text: was it too long, too complex, did it use the right language, was it accessible and inclusive, and was it addressing different people with diverse needs and experiences?

The museum also changed its attitude to internal and external space. It looked back at its history as a finite enclosed structure that used didactic methods to direct, to teach, and to reinforce traditional messages, and introduced within this traditional structure, new internal spaces that were fluid, flexible, and playful. The Turbine Hall at Tate Modern became a space that was able to house massive sculptures ... or nothing but sound, interesting juxtapositions of work across time, high towers, cracks in the foundation, shining suns, and exhilarating slides and visitors loved to come and be part of these experiences.

The idea that attitudes become form is in no way, new. This is how society changes. Laws that ultimately govern us, were, at one time, simple changes of attitude. But attitudes that become form in the art museum are not just about laws and rules, although there will inevitably be times when what we collect and how we store and display our collections, will depend on law. Attitudes that become the form of art museums are about culture and heritage, about how we see ourselves, how we value art, what we say and what we write about art, what we know and what we have chosen not to know, and how we redress a historic imbalance of gender, race, and ethnicity both in the collections that we have, the new acquisitions that we make, and the visitors that we are hoping to attract.

Changes of attitude in the way in which museums market, manage, and identify themselves may be difficult … but they are possible. But changes of attitude get stuck when they come up against history and legacy. Some parts of our permanent collection includes work that we used to cherish so dearly and that we believed to be our national treasure, work that once defined our values, our heritage, and our beliefs but now looks tired, outmoded, and unfashionable. Permanence is no longer highly valued, and we must decide whether we are happy for choices that were made on our behalf in very different times, may still be used as a reflection of modern values and ideals.

It is this final issue that provokes most unrest for the museum, a place that has always had at its heart, longevity, permanence, and a commitment to creating legacy. Debates about ownership, legacy, and repatriation are now critical for how we see the future. Museums have entered a period of epistemological uncertainty and the foundations upon which they were built, their stability, longevity, institutional confidence, and shared legacy is under scrutiny. This is a moment when frameworks of knowledge and meaning are being scrutinised and traditional values and institutional identity, challenged. This is a moment of doubt in the sustainability and continual expansion of the permanent collection and unease regarding the desirability (or possibility) of material objects becoming *permanent* signifiers of the passing of time

This is a moment when we need to think of ways of lifting the historic cloud that has settled over what we thought of as a proud legacy but now leaves us doubting so much. This is a time of urgency when we must re-evaluate, re-vision, and repurpose collections, text, and the museum space and reconsider how we deal with a legacy that will be forever 'ours'.

Index

aesthetic 9
Alemani, Cecilia 70
Ammann, Jean-Christophe 7
Angerstein, John Julius 10
art criticism 62
art history 8–10, 31, 42, 47, 56, 57, 60, 62, 67; aesthetics 9; conventional centring 69; nationalism 70; twentieth century 17
The Art Museum in Modern Times (Saumarez Smith) 56
Art Museum of Chicago 20
Arts Council England (ACE) 65
art writing 61–62

Bacon, Francis 35, 65
Bal, Mieke 35
Balshaw, Maria 7
Baltimore Museum 65
Barr, Alfred 7, 35
Barthes, Roland 36
Baudelaire, Charles 6
Bauman, Zygmunt 21, 22
Belting, Hans 19
Bennett, Tony 6
Bingham, Juliet 49
The Birth of the Museum (Bennett) 6
Bishop, Claire 22
Bourdieu, Pierre 6, 15, 31
Bourgeois, Louise 49, 50, 51, 55
BP 31, 70
breathing space 16, 57
British Museum 10, 63, 64, 70
Bryson, Norman 34, 41
Button, Virginia 14

cabinet of curiosity 6, 10, 12, 17, 22, 30, 48
caption, 9; expanded caption, 9
Carsten Höller 49
Century City 14
collaborative creativity 23
colonialism 67
Colston, Edward 21
conceptual art movements 16
convivial community 23
cultural capital 7, 15, 62
culture of lifestyle 19
curator 8, 12, 14, 15, 17, 18, 32, 37; co-curating 19; curating 14, 15; curatorial turn 11; individual curator 18, 20; individual curating 24
Cuno, James 66

Danto, Arthur 35
DCMS (Department for Digital, Culture, Media & Sport) 7
decolonisation 63; decolonial activism 67–68
Decolonization is not a metaphor (Eve Tuck and K. Wayne Yang) 4
deconstructive turn 11
de Duve, Thierry 9
Dercon, Chris 7
Derrida, Jacques 15
De Salva, Donna 49
disinterestedness 40
Double Bind (Munoz) 49

Eastlake, Charles Sir 10
Eliasson, Olafur 49, 54

Index

Elkins, James 9
empty space 16, 53, 57
encyclopaedic collection 8, 20
Endt, Marion 11
Engage 61
Ensslin, Felix 4, 15, 60
Enwezor, Okwui 70
epistemology 7; epistemological uncertainty 11, 33, 41, 55, 77; epistemological methodology 62; epistemological turn 11
Esche, Charles 14
exhibition space 4, 12, 16, 56, 60; exhibitions 13, 20

Fanon, Frantz 71
Ferguson, Bruce 50
Fischer, Hartwig 64
Foucault, Michel 4, 6, 23, 51, 54
Foucauldian interpretation 60
Frege, Gottlob 37

Gayford, Martin 46
Gem (The Group for Education in Museums) 65
Gero, Robert 9
The Glance of Infinity (Horn) 50
Global Art Forum 62
Greenberg, Reesa 17, 18
Gumbrecht, Hans Ulrich 37, 38

Hall, Stuart 38
heterotopias 4, 23, 45, 55
heterotopic space 6, 45, 54, 55, 57, 60
Hicks, Dan 64
Hirsch, E.D. Jr. 40, 41
Hoffman, Jens 16
Höller, Carsten 49, 52, 54
Hölz, Marjatta 12
Horniman Museum 65
Horn, Rebecca 50
Hultén, Pontus 12
Hunt, Tristram 64
Hyundai 48

ideology 11
I Do, I Undo, I Redo (Bourgeois) 49, 50
inclusivity 22, 33
individual curating 18–24
inequality 69
institutional interpretation 15, 36
institutional text 32
institutional judgment 7
International Council of Museums 20
interpretation, 2, 8, 9, 21, 30, 33, 39; interpreter 39; interpretative text 4, 30, 33, 34; interpretative strategies, 36; *Interpretation, Theory and the Encounter* (Tate Britain 2010 conference)
intersectionality 68

Johnson, Boris 66
Joule, Barry 65

Kabakov, Ilya 54
Kapoor, Anish 49
Kant Immanuel 9, 40
Kihara, Yuki 71
Krauss, Rosalind 8, 31, 47
Krens, Thomas 8
Kunsthalle Bern 7, 16

legacy 12, 20, 23, 61
Levete, Amanda 56
Lichtenstein, Roy 65
Live In Your Head: When Attitude Becomes Form 16
Liquid Modernity (Bauman) 21
literary perspectives 40–41

MacGregor, Neil 3
Macron, Emmanuel 63
Mailloux, Steven 39
Masai, Judith 13
May, Susan 49
Matisse, Henri 34
Merleau-Ponty, Maurice 51
methodology 11
Metropolitan Museum of Art 47
minimalism 14
Mitchell, W.J.T 40
modernism 10, 13, 24
modernity: Baudelaire's definition of 6; digital 11; identity 11; liquid 11; Modernism 10
Modern Art Oxford 2
modern museum 6, 22, 23, 45, 55, 56, 75

Morgan, Jessica 49
Morris, Frances 9, 12
Moxley Keith 36, 38
Munoz, Juan 49
museum curating 6, 20–21
museum interpretations 30–42
museum label 33, 39
Museum of Contemporary Art (MCA) 12
Museum of Modern Art (MoMA) 2, 7, 8, 65
Museums After Modernism (Masai) 13
Museums Journal 66
Museums Association 65
museum space 11, 16, 23, 41, 45–57, 60, 76, 77
museum text 30–42, 62, 76

Natalie Bell building, Tate Modern 69
National Gallery 1, 3, 10, 47
National Portrait Gallery 1
Nauman, Bruce 49
New Displays 3, 9, 31, 32
newsreaders, 36–37
non-hierarchical social model 23

Obrist, Hans Ulrich 12, 15, 16, 18
Oval Gallery 56

permanent collection 8, 11, 24
personal curating 19
Perl, Jed 47
pop art 14
post-colonial theory 67
postmodernism 11, 13; postmodernist thinking 10
Postmodernism's Museum Without Walls (Krauss) 47
Preziosi, Donald 40, 41
public museum 7, 10, 18, 30

Race Equality Taskforce 69
remembering, act of 17
reparation 66
repatriation 66
replica, riff, reprise 23
restitution 66
rest space 56
resurrection, act of 17
Ricœur, Paul 36, 38
Rondeau, James 20

room panel, 9
Royal Museums Greenwich 70

Said, Edward 30, 34, 66
Sainsbury Gallery 56
Salcedo, Doris 49, 55
Saumarez Smith, Charles 56
Science Museum Group 70
Sehgal, Tino 49, 53
Serota, Nicholas 2, 3, 8, 9, 31, 49, 56
Sharjah Art Foundation (2021) 66
Shibboleth (Salcedo) 49, 55
signification 15
Sloane, Hans Sir 10, 63
social act 18–24
Sorrell, Beverley 33
Soueif, Ahdaf 70
Soundscapes (Nauman) 49
spatial choreography 16
spatial forms/distances 51–52
Stevenson Dennis 31
Sunflower Seeds (Weiwei) 49
surrealism 14
Sylvester, David 35
Szeemann, Harald 1, 7, 16, 17

Tate, Henry Sir 10
Tate 1, 69, 70, 76; Tate Gallery 2
Tate Modern 7, 14, 31, 46–49; acquisition policy 9; practical and ideological spaces 47; slavery 10; Turbine Hall 4, 45, 46, 48, 54, 56, 60, 76
temporary exhibitions 12–18
Test Site (Höller) 49, 52
text 30, 33, 39, 41, 42, 61, 62, 76; text-based interpretation 45
These Associations (Sehgal) 49, 53
The Art Museum in Modern Times (Saumarez Smith) 56
traffic space 56
transition uncertainty 11
Tuck, Eve 4, 67
Turner Prize 14
Tuttle Richard 31

Über Sinn und Bedeuting [Sense and Reference] (Frege) 37
uncertainty: epistemological 11, 33, 55, 77; transition 11
Unilever 49–50

Venice Biennale 70
Verges, Françoise 66, 69
Victoria and Albert Museum 1

Wallace Collection 63
wall text/panels 9, 33, 39
Washington National Gallery 47
Weather Project (Eliasson) 49, 54
Weiwei, Ai 49
When Attitudes Become Form 1, 16

When Attitudes become Form become Attitudes 17
Whitechapel Gallery 2
Williams, Jonathan 64
Wilson, David 64
Wilson, Simon 32
Windsor, Mark 52
written interpretation 37, 38, 41
Wunderkammer, 6

Yang, K. Wayne 4, 67

For Product Safety Concerns and Information please contact our EU
representative GPSR@taylorandfrancis.com
Taylor & Francis Verlag GmbH, Kaufingerstraße 24, 80331 München, Germany

www.ingramcontent.com/pod-product-compliance
Lightning Source LLC
Chambersburg PA
CBHW051800230426
43670CB00012B/2364